Praise for
A Message from Garcia

"Having written twelve books in the field of personal motivation over the past three decades, I have great appreciation for that rare and exceptional author whose book is so rich in uncommon wisdom and clearheaded guidance that it has the power to impact virtually every life it touches. Charlie Garcia's *A Message from Garcia* is at the head of the list."

—Shad Helmstetter, Ph.D. Best-selling author of *What To Say When You Talk to Yourself* and *Who Are You Really and What Do You Want?*

"How do you build a world-class company and find happiness at the same time? Charles Garcia teaches readers in a lighthearted fun way; how they can achieve anything they want by applying proven success strategies."

—Marcia Israel-Curley, *Los Angeles Times* "Woman of the Year" who built Judy's from a tiny woman's clothing store to a major public company with 104 stores and 2,000 employees; author of *Defying the Odds: Sharing the Lessons I Learned as a Pioneer Entrepreneur*

"When you finish reading this amazing book you will have all the keys to success at your fingertips. Destined to become a classic, it is a must read for leaders, educators, parents, and especially for anyone whom children turn to for advice and direction."

—Major General Clifford L. Stanley (ret.) was responsible for education and training in the entire U.S. Marine Corps serving as one of the highest ranking African-Americans in the military. He is currently the Chief Operating Officer, University of Pennsylvania.

"We often get bogged down in all the reasons why we can't do something, why we can't get ahead or succeed—this is particularly true for minorities. Anyone, regardless of race, creed, or color can succeed, and if you don't believe me, read Charlie Garcia's book, it can be your success bible."

—Tommy Hodingh, CEO, MagRabbit, Inc. Tommy was named the 2003 "Asian Entrepreneur of the Year" by *Asian Enterprise* magazine *and* the Asian Business Association; and in 2001 the "National Minority Business Enterprise of the Year" by the National Minority Supplier Diversity Council.

"Charles Garcia invites the reader to take the reins of life. There is no more life-affirming message than the reminder that this is your life, your chance. Embrace it, dare to dream, and know that all the necessary tools for success are within you. This is the building block of learning and *A Message from Garcia* is an essential dose of inspiration."

—Eduardo J. Padron, President, Miami-Dade Community College, the largest multi-campus two-year college in the nation.

"Charles Garcia is one who can walk his talk, he is a doer, not just a motivational guy. With quite a bit of humorous anecdotes *A Message from Garcia* is a joy to read. It will certainly put a smile on your face, a glow in your heart, and a success halo around your life."

—Frank McKinney, best-selling author of *Make it BIG!*
49 Secrets for Building a Life of Extreme Success

"Having come from a very poor family I understand first hand the many hurdles some of us have that may make achieving goals, or even great success, seemingly impossible. I discovered that if one remains positive and committed to their dream, success is definitely possible. Charlie Garcia's book shows us all how we can overcome hurdles and rise to the success to which every person aspires."

—Bill Yost, legendary football coach profiled in the movie
Remember the Titans

"So many of our students have goals and dreams, but unfortunately they are often unclear and unfocused. *A Message from Garcia* is a great book for college students. It can help them discover their passion, while providing inspiration and practical advice to help them achieve whatever they want. This book teaches students things they will never learn in school!"

—Professor Arnold A. Heggestad, Director, Center for
Entrepreneurship and Innovation, the University of Florida

"*A Message from Garcia* can help you finally, once and for all, find out what you are good at, what you love, what you are passionate about, and lead you toward a more satisfying, rewarding, and fulfilling life."

—Mark Victor Hansen, coauthor, #1 *New York Times* bestseller *Chicken Soup for the Soul.*

"Garcia's book is a unique blend of techniques to leverage external opportunities by recognizing and developing internal strengths—a must read, not only for entrepreneurs but for anyone with goals and dreams to achieve."

—Professor Steven Stralser, Global Entrepreneurship Center, Thunderbird: The American Graduate School of International Management

"*A Message from Garcia* is a riveting book filled with exciting stories and clear strategies that will set you on a sure path to success if you follow its powerful principles."

—Joseph B. Anderson Jr., his heroic actions were featured in the 1967 academy award-winning documentary *The Anderson Platoon* about the infantry platoon he commanded in Vietnam. He now leads as CEO, Vibration Control Technologies, one of the 100 largest black-owned industrial businesses in the nation.

"Charles Garcia could be Jack Ryan's character in a Tom Clancy novel— part action hero, part public servant, part world class entrepreneur. You should read this book slowly because it's packed with pearls of wisdom cultivated by studying powerful mentors and applying that knowledge to achieve extraordinary success."

—Jay Rifenbary, national speaker and best-selling author of *No Excuse!—Key Principles for Balancing Life & Achieving Success*

"Charles Garcia challenges young people to dream big and pursue what they truly love. Whether they want to run a marathon or run a company, or pursue something totally out of the ordinary, *A Message from Garcia* offers powerful action strategies that anyone, at any age, can follow to achieve their dreams."

>—Jennifer Kushell, *New York Times* best-selling author of *Secrets of the Young & Successful: How to Get Everything You Want Without Waiting a Lifetime*

"In less than six years, Charlie Garcia built one of the nation's fastest growing companies in America. *A Message from Garcia* captures many valuable lessons for everyone, especially how to create your own 'success compass'—a brilliant, yet simple technique that can literally change the course of your life."

>—Don Kelin, CEO, CADDO Design & Office Products, Inc. Don received the National Indian Business Owner of the Year Award; the U.S. Department of Commerce National Minority Supplier of the Year Award; and is the Chairman of the Board of Directors, National Center for American Indian Enterprise Development.

"As a lifelong educator, I have dedicated my life to creating programs and curriculum that help prepare students for life. *A Message from Garcia* is an extraordinary book that teaches children things they don't learn in school—things that are as important as math and reading—because it will give them the knowledge and tools they need to succeed."

>—Dr. Art Johnson, Superintendent of Palm Beach County Schools, the 14th largest district in the nation.

"Commitment and perseverance are essential to achieving your goals, and nowhere is that more important than when you decide to lose weight and improve your health. *A Message from Garcia* will help give people the mental stamina, energy, and focus to do whatever they want, including improving their health."

>—Larry North, fitness expert and best-selling author of *Larry North's Slimdown for Life*

A Message from Garcia

Yes, You Can Succeed

CHARLES P. GARCIA

WILEY

John Wiley & Sons, Inc.

Published by John Wiley & Sons, Inc., Hoboken, New Jersey
Published simultaneously in Canada

For general information on our other products and services, or technical support, please contact our Customer Care Department within the United States at 800-762-2974, outside the United States at 317-572-3993 or fax 317-572-4002.

Wiley also publishes its books in a variety of electronic formats. Some content that appears in print may not be available in electronic books.

For more information about Wiley products, visit our web site at www.wiley.com.

ISBN 0-471-44893-1

Printed in the United States of America

10 9 8 7 6 5 4 3

*This book is dedicated to all of you
with the courage to nurture your dreams,
to keep the flames of hope alive,
and persevere in the face of
overwhelming obstacles*

Acknowledgments

SOMEONE ONCE SAID THAT THERE IS NO LIMIT TO WHAT YOU CAN accomplish, as long as you are willing to let someone else get the credit. This book was brought to life with the help and support of many people. I am overwhelmed by the feelings I have towards so many dedicated family members, friends, and co-workers who have made this book possible.

To my wife, Allison, who showed me the world in color, when I saw it only in black and white. She made me realize that life with a woman who loves you is the closest thing to heaven you can find on earth.

To my late father, Dr. Carlos A. Garcia, and my mother, Marilyn McCarthy Garcia, words are not enough to describe the love and care that you put into making me who I am.

To my three children—Olivia, Sterling, and Paloma—and my brother, Brian, and sisters, Ginger and Colleen, your love is my joy and my strength.

To Jeff Mustard who joined in my vision of helping to complete a book that would positively change the lives of those who read it. This book could not have been completed without his dedication.

To Les Abromovitz for his invaluable thoughts about the book's organization and focus, and especially for his thoughtful research and editing of each chapter as the book progressed.

To my editor, Debra Englander, of John Wiley & Sons, for her important feedback, encouragement, and support, you are a true professional and a pleasure to work with.

To Virginia Garcia de Chacin who shaped the marketing strategy, unselfishly giving her time and feedback, and sharing her upbeat nature and good humor.

To my business partners Alexis Korybut and John Curry who are the backbone of Sterling Financial. Alexis' talent is only eclipsed by his extraordinary sense of integrity, and John the consummate team player is the most consistent businessman I know.

To some of my dear friends: Jorge Arrizurieta, Brad Baker, Sylvia Bayon, Ellen Birkman, George Burden, Kevin Carreno, Lee-En Chung, Jorge Dominicis, Lance Frank, Norma Garza, Mark Hagemen, George Herrera, Marc Holtzman, Art Johnson, Nancy Kelley, Mark Klein, Mitch Maidique, Myles Martel, Eduardo Padron, Mike Ramos, Marty Rauch, Cliff Stanley, Robert Staples, and Pete Wehner; I treasure each of your unique contributions. Your sense of humor and wisdom pulled me across the bumpy roads and I am eternally grateful.

For my new friends in the Center for Entrepreneurship and Innovation, the Florida Hispanic 100, the Florida State Board of Education, Leadership Florida, the National Minority Supplier Development Council, the Sterling Financial family, The Executive Committee (TEC), the U.S. Air Force Academy Association of Graduates, the U.S. Hispanic Chamber of Commerce, the White House Fellows, and the Young President's Organization (YPO); thank you for your friendship and inspiration. I look forward to a long adventurous journey.

To the officers and enlisted personnel from all four branches of the armed forces with whom I have served and worked over the years, you have earned my deep respect.

To my many mentors and leaders who shaped my beliefs and values, the giants upon whose shoulders I stand, including: William J. Bennett, Governor Jeb Bush, Jaime Escalante, General John R. Galvin (ret.), Seymour Holtzman, John Lombardi, Omar Torrijos, and John C. Whitehead; I thank you for your wise counsel and for your faith in me.

And finally, I thank God, my cosmic companion, who has been profoundly real to me and who in the midst of all my setbacks has given me an inner calm to transform dark yesterdays into bright tomorrows.

Contents

PART THREE

Success Strategy 1: Dream Big

121

PART FOUR

Success Strategy 2: Start Planning Now
159

PART FIVE

Success Strategy 3: Take Action
185

Contents

PART SIX

Success Strategy 4: Persevere

231

Foreword

ANYONE WHO HAS HEARD ME SPEAK OR IS FAMILIAR WITH MY WORK AS A teacher from the movie *Stand and Deliver* knows that I don't believe in taking no as an answer. When students say they can't possibly take advanced calculus, I say, "why not?" When teens say they don't expect to go onto college because no one in their family has ever done so, again I say, "why not?"

Charles Garcia shares a similar view. While Charlie was fortunate enough to come from a family of professionals who encouraged and supported his educational efforts, his philosophy matches mine. After serving in the military, holding government positions, and training to become an attorney, Charlie realized that he needed to do something else. Turning his back on a potentially lucrative legal career, Charles started to build his own business from scratch.

Today, six years after starting his firm in a tiny office with just two employees, Sterling Financial is on solid footing. Charlie could certainly spend more time with his family and focus on his business. But he chooses instead to devote an enormous amount of his time, energy, resources, and money to a cause that he feels strongly about, a cause that he is passionate about—education. It is through these efforts that I have come to know Charles Garcia and to respect him for all he is doing for the greater cause of education. Through an appointment by Governor Jeb Bush to Florida's State Board of Education and President George W. Bush's appointment to the Commission on Educational Excellence for Hispanic Americans, a commission on which I also serve, Charlie demonstrates by both word and deed his concern for helping others, particularly young Hispanics, to help them make their dreams a reality.

This book chronicles Charlie's career, from establishing his first office in the broom closet of another firm, to its rise as the fastest growing Hispanic company in the United States. But the book is much more than a tale of success, it is a book that is a testament to the importance of finding one's true calling in life and combining that piece of self discovery with strategies to pursue one's own desires, dreams, and goals. A keen observer, Charlie employed principles he learned from many successful people he worked with to help grow his firm into an international success. Along the way, he found his heart in a place that has enabled him to make this world better by improving educational opportunities for children and touching the hearts of man. Today, Charlie has a voice as a policy maker at both the State and National levels which provides him a platform to make a difference in the lives of children and the education they receive in America.

What inspired Charlie? As a child, his father read *A Message to Garcia* to him. This book, first published in 1899, discusses the fearless efforts of one man during the Spanish-American War. Rowan, a messenger, risked his life to carry a message to Garcia, leader of the insurgents. Rowan took the initiative, going well beyond his duties, without being asked to. This is an important part of Charlie's message: It takes extra effort to do something without being asked; showing initiative is perhaps the best strategy to get ahead.

This book is more than inspiring; it is a handbook that can be used by virtually anyone who wants something more out of life. It should be read by people who are not sure what it is they want out of life or how to get it.

I have learned that education is power and can change lives. Just as education can change a child's life, the information and knowledge that can be learned by reading this book can also be life-altering. To have a rewarding and satisfying life one must have a burning desire to succeed, what is referred to in Spanish as *ganas*. To succeed you must have both *ganas* and passion. Charlie has found his passion and now he shares with you how you can find yours.

Hopefully, this book will ignite your *ganas*, and will propel you toward your passion so you too can discover your true calling in life, and will lead you toward a more satisfying and rewarding future for you and your family.

—Jaime Escalante, May 2003

PART ONE

GET BUSY LIVING
OR
GET BUSY DYING

CHAPTER 1

···

Babe Ruth: Strikeout King or Home Run King?

I WAS WAITING FOR A CAB TO THE AIRPORT. WHEN IT ARRIVED, THE driver hopped out and greeted me in English, but spoke with a thick Spanish accent. I automatically responded to him in Spanish. With my 5-foot 10-inch height, light brown hair, and green eyes, I'm sure he was startled by my fluency. I had my favorite travel bag, the one with the scuffs, nicks, and the remnants of destination sticker glue. I also had my surfboard, which of course had surprised the driver.

"Why don't we strap it on top of the roof?" I asked in Spanish, as I pulled out the cable restraints I've used so many times before. Without too much trouble, we got the board secured. I am accustomed to riding short boards that are more maneuverable for the kind of small waves commonly found in Florida. My 9-foot bright orange and green surfboard is called a long board and it's built for riding big waves, the kind I was hopefully going to meet.

I turned to hug my wife and children. Allison, my wife of 10 years, whom I met when I was a White House Fellow in Washington, D.C., gave me a big hug and a kiss, while my two children, Olivia, 9, and Sterling, 7, competed for my attention. My third child, Paloma, 1, was not born yet. Allison was a great sport about my leaving during the holidays. She understood how important it was for me to go on this trip. I kissed the kids and hopped into the cab.

"Señor, donde vamos?" inquired the cabbie as he pulled away from the curb.

"Aero puerto de Miami," I responded, settling into the back seat. I turned around and looked at my family one last time.

The best way to get to Hawaii from Boca Raton is through Miami International Airport. I was very excited about this trip because surfing means a lot to me. I learned to surf while growing up in Panama. I hadn't surfed much over the past 20 years, and this trip would be special. On New Year's Day, the first day of the new millennium, I planned to be surfing in Kauai, one of Hawaii's main islands. I closed my eyes. I already could hear the waves, feel the sand under my feet, and smell the ocean.

When we arrived at the airport, a porter took my board, gave me a receipt, and disappeared into the back, or wherever it is that they take surfboards, probably alongside bicycles, golf bags, skis, and all the other unwieldy stuff people bring along on vacations. I grabbed my bag and headed to the check-in counter. I took my place in line and had barely put down my bag when my cell phone rang. I glanced at the number in the phone display—a 305 area code—obviously someone in Miami, but I didn't recognize the number.

"Charles Garcia," I said. That's how I usually answer the phone when I don't recognize the number. The voice on the other end was pleasant, yet I didn't recognize it any more than the number.

"Hello, Mr. Garcia," she said with an upbeat note.

"Yes, how can I help you?" I asked as I leaned forward, grabbed my bag, and moved up one space in line.

"Mr. Garcia, this is Sylvia Bayon. I'm a producer with Univision Television, and I'd like to congratulate you."

"Really?" I said, a bit startled and not knowing what she was talking about. "What for?"

"Univision Television has chosen to feature you in a series that spotlights Hispanic role models who have made an exceptional impact on the culture and life of American society," she said, even more enthusiastically.

"Univision Television," I thought, "Yeah, right." I was sure that friends were playing a trick on me and were waiting for me to bite on this, hook, line, and sinker.

"Miss Babalon," I said, intentionally mispronouncing her name, "you actually had me for a moment, but go ahead and tell my friends I'm not buying it. Tell them to have a Happy New Year and I'll see them in the new millennium."

While they would probably be nursing hangovers and popping aspirin, I would be riding the surf in Hawaii on New Year's Day. I hung up and laughed to myself, "Nice try." I have lived in a lot of interesting places, including the Republic of Panama, Colorado, Honduras, Ecuador, Washington, D.C., New York, and Florida. I have maintained many friendships with people I have met on my travels, and we often play pranks on each other. It was probably one of these friends behind this phone call.

The phone rang again. "Mr. Garcia?"

"Yes?"

"Sylvia Bayon, again."

"Look, Miss Biddle, thanks for calling, but please tell my friends I'm onto them. It's really not a good time to chat; I'm standing in line at Miami airport on my way to Hawaii." I hung up the phone again. "Wow, what a bunch of nuts." I checked my watch; I had about a half-hour to kill.

I made my way through the concourse and stopped at one of the bookstores. I always stop at the bookstores. I read at least two books a week, usually biographies or business topics. I browsed the business section but reminded myself that I was going to be on vacation, so I reluctantly started to look at some novels and magazines. I chose a Robert Ludlum thriller, but I couldn't resist picking up a dozen news and business magazines. After all, it's a long flight, and the Ludlum novel was the perfect counterbalance.

I was on my way out of the store when the phone rang again. It was the same 305 number, so I answered without stopping.

"Look, Mr. Garcia, *please* do not hang up the phone," said the voice, considerably more high-pitched and definitely tinged with a hint of annoyance.

"Yes, Miss Babalon, how can I help you?"

"Mr. Garcia, it's Bayon, Sylvia Bayon, not Babalon or Biddle, and I don't know what you think is going on, but I am a producer with Univision Television and I want to talk to you about featuring you in our series *Orgullo Hispano.*" (This is pronounced, Or-gu-yo Is-pan-o, which means Hispanic Pride.)

"Uh huh, Miss Bayon, and what exactly do you do with this Or-gu-yo Is-pan-o?" I asked, slowly exaggerating the name with a heavy American accent, still a bit smug, but considerably less so than before. Gee, what would happen if she really was a producer with Univision, the world's most watched Spanish language television network, with more than 120 million viewers? Well, I guess she'd think I was an idiot.

"Basically, we'd like to come to your office with a television crew and film you for the day. Then we'll cut a 30-second television commercial, a promotional piece, a sort of mini-biography that we will air every day for the next three years to our worldwide television audience."

That got my attention. I stopped walking to continue the conversation. "Miss Bayon," I said, and I made sure to get her name right this time, "who else have you featured?"

"Well, let me see," she said. "Singer Ricky Martin, boxer Oscar De la Hoya, math teacher Jaime Escalante, actress Salma Hayek, and baseball star Sammy Sosa, to name a few."

"That's quite an impressive group of people, although quite frankly, I really don't see where I fit in." I was greeted with silence. I don't think anyone ever questioned why they were chosen for this series. I suppose the people who were selected are so high profile that they don't question it.

"Let me go over my notes." She then proceeded to rattle off a list of accomplishments.

Then she came to her final question. "Is it also true that you founded a company with three people in a cleaned-out broom closet of another firm, and now you have over 60 offices in seven countries?"

"All that's true," I responded, "But did your research uncover all the major screwups I've had along the way?"

"Screwups?" she asked inquisitively.

"Do you know much about baseball, Miss Bayon?" I asked.

"A little."

"Do you know that Babe Ruth was not only the Home Run King, but he led the league in strikeouts? Nolan Ryan, the retired pitcher, is baseball's Strikeout King, but he also led the league in the number of bases given up on balls."

"Mr. Garcia, I'm sure you're right, but most people only remember Babe Ruth for his home runs, and pitcher Nolan Ryan for his strikeouts," she said. Dismissing my pithy baseball analogy, she pressed on. "Look, Mr. Garcia," she continued. "We're looking to feature a businessman in our next spotlight, especially one committed to the Hispanic community, and we are intrigued with your success and the fact that you're not even 40 years old."

Did she have to mention my age? When people do that, I like to remind them that Napoleon conquered Europe before the age of 30—and how that was a *real* achievement. In any event, I held my tongue since she batted my previous one-liner into oblivion. I glanced at my watch again. People were hurrying to their gates, and I should be one of them.

"We think you'd make a great role model for our series," she said. "You know, Mr. Garcia, you should think about writing a book some day."

"Well, I don't know about writing a book, but I am at the airport and I'm about to board a plane. What would you like to do next, Miss Bayon?"

"I'll let you go and I'll call you when you get back so we can set it up."

"Sounds great," I said, and I hung up the phone. As I went off to my gate, I was replaying the conversation in my mind. She probably thought I was a jerk. After all, I did hang up on her twice. I'm sure she had a pretty good story to tell her friends back at the office.

"Can you believe it?" I could hear her telling her colleagues. "I called this guy Garcia to be on Orgullo Hispano and he hung up on me, twice. He thought it was a friend playing a joke on him" I could hear the laughter. "Interesting guy, but what an idiot."

Find What
You Love to Do,
Even If It's Selling
Shower Curtains

I FOUND MY WAY TO SEAT 4A AND QUICKLY GLANCED AT THE PERSON who would be sitting next to me for the next 12 hours. He was a short bald man, in his mid 50s, wearing a bright green sport coat, who reminded me of Danny DeVito.

I tucked my book in the pocket of the seat in front of me and put my hand out and introduced myself. "Charles Garcia," I said.

"Clarence Kodner," he replied sharply with a bit of a southern drawl. Very quickly, I learned that Clarence was a salesman. He sold shower curtains and was on his way to Hawaii for a "grand annual worldwide" shower curtain convention of some sort. Clarence lived in Atlanta and had been in Miami calling on some supermarket chain clients, and was now off to network with his shower curtain comrades.

Even before the plane took off, I learned more about the shower curtain business than you could imagine. It's more interesting than you might expect. I discovered that there are different gauges of plastic, that design elements need to be considered, and that curtains can even offer an antifungal capability.

I looked out the window and began to drift a little. I started thinking about Sylvia Bayon. I thought about her remark, the one she made just before hanging up the phone. "You know, you should write a book." When she mentioned it, I dismissed it, because the interview was the main agenda. But as it came back to me, I started to reflect on it.

Could I write a book on success?

Lost in thought, I mulled over the fact that I studied leadership at the Air Force Academy where I served as Chairman of the Cadet Wing Honor Committee, and I was later apprenticed to some exceptional people. For several years I worked as a key assistant to General John Galvin, a four-star General who went on to become the NATO Supprem Allied Commander. Beyond General Galvin, as a White House Fellow I worked as a Special Assistant to former Secretary of Education and drug czar William Bennett, and John Whitehead, the former Chairman of Goldman Sachs. There was also Buzzy Schwartz, perhaps the best trader on Wall Street. There was also my father-in-law Seymour Holtzman, a brilliant businessman. In 1960, at age 26, he took his first company public. I worked for Seymour for three years and learned a great deal from him. What could I offer to someone interested in achieving success? Could I somehow convey the important lessons I learned from my mentors and other unusual characters I met in my various positions? If you're a high-profile CEO who has a household name, you've got credibility and people are more likely to want to hear what you have to say. But, can a reader learn about leadership, success, or for that matter, anything from physical fitness to better relationships, from people who are not celebrities? Although I wasn't really sure about the phone call from Sylvia Bayon, if she wanted to profile me, maybe I *could* inspire people to achieve their maximum potential.

I glanced at my watch, a Rolex, a gift from my father. It had been given to him by the wife of General Omar Torrijos, the charismatic leader of Panama who negotiated the Panama Canal treaties with President Jimmy Carter. My father was a Georgetown University–trained heart surgeon who became Surgeon General of Panama. Over time, my father became a trusted adviser to Torrijos. When Torrijos died in a plane crash, his widow gave my father the watch he was wearing that fateful day. To me it's more than a timepiece; it is a true piece of history with tremendous sentimental value. I also thought of my mother, who for 22 years taught in the public schools as a seventh-grade science teacher. I learned a great deal from both my parents.

I *can* write a book on success, I thought.

The rest of the flight to Hawaii with Clarence was uneventful. I read, he ate and drank. Now and again he'd point out some remarkable new shower curtain fact, including the mesmerizing world of rods and rings that make up the "shower curtain" package. I was actually fascinated by the business and there was no doubt that Clarence was good at what he did, which was one of the reasons why Clarence was flying first class. Not only was he good at what he did, but he was passionate about it; and that translated to his excellence in a remarkably mundane field. He was obviously a superb shower curtain salesman.

I began to think about what kind of book I would write. I would want it to help people looking for a way to improve their performance and also for people who are unhappy and "looking for something more out of life." Most importantly, I would want my book to be useful to people trying to figure out what direction their lives should take. I would want it to help them learn more about themselves and how to discover their strengths.

I started to scribble a few notes on some cocktail napkins. As we were flying at 35,000 feet, some key ideas began to emerge.

Napkin Note I: Define Success

I believe that to achieve success you must find your calling in life and pursue it regardless of financial gain. Richness and true happiness in life can be achieved by having a job that you love or simply by being passionate at whatever it is that you choose to do.

Napkin Note 2:
Success Does Not Equal Money

You don't have to be rich to be successful. Success does not equate to how much money you have in the bank. Success is about finding your calling in life, and doing it regardless of how much money you make or what other people think. Depending upon what you love to do, you might have the potential to make a lot of money, but that's a function of the type of job or career that you choose to pursue.

Napkin Note 3:
Help People Find Their Calling

Helping people to find their calling in life
would be an extraordinary accomplishment.
My book would offer two tests that people can
take to find their calling. One is based on the
most widely utilized personality preference
instrument in the world, which helps explain
your personality type. The other shows your
five innate strengths and provides a tool for
you to tap into your true potential.

Napkin Note 4:
Not a Psychobabble Feel-Good Book

This book would not be designed to make
you feel good about yourself, nor would it
be a get-rich-quick-overnight book. The
book would provide lessons to help those
who applied them to succeed at whatever
they choose to do. That is not to say that it
will be easy. Success requires commitment
and attention.

Napkin Note 5: Success Beliefs

We all make certain assumptions that shape almost everything we do. Some of these beliefs help us to become successful, whereas others hold us down like chains around our ankles. <u>Success beliefs</u> are powerful magnets that attract success and I have seen them used by all of the successful people with whom I have apprenticed. My book would help people activate these mental magnets so they can attract success.

Napkin Note 6: Success Strategies

Since we are not born with a road map showing us the path to success, we have to learn what I call <u>success strategies.</u> Think of a strategy as the answer to <u>where</u> you are going and <u>how</u> you are going to get there. I observed these strategies while apprenticing for some extraordinarily successful leaders in the military, in government, and in business. I applied this knowledge to my own business and crystallized this knowledge down to four simple strategies, which would be a big part of my book.

Napkin Note 7: ~~Take Action~~
Get Busy Living or Get Busy Dying

My book would provide readers a detailed
road map on how to achieve success. However,
none of it works unless you take action. Many
times people have a great plan and know
exactly what they need to do, but they
don't follow through. Don't be one of those
unhappy people who procrastinate and let
their dreams slip away.

Eventually, I ran out of napkins so I decided to close my eyes and rest for a while. I reached for the headphones, thinking that I'd drown out Clarence's snoring with the movie that was playing. I fumbled with the earphone jack, turned the volume way up, and heard Morgan Freeman's familiar voice. When I looked up at the screen, I recognized the movie, too, the Oscar-winning film *The Shawshank Redemption*. The scene playing on the screen that moment struck a chord. Morgan Freeman's character, Red, gave this piece of life-altering advice to Tim Robbins, who plays Andy Dufresne, a man imprisoned for life for a crime he didn't commit. Red says to Andy, "Either get busy living or get busy dying."

Andy takes Red's advice to heart and develops a strategy to achieve his dream of freedom. He sets his strategy in motion, and every single day, quietly and unknown to anyone else, including the audience, he takes action to achieve his dream. Andy uses a tiny geological specimen hammer, small enough to be hidden in his Bible, to tunnel through tons of rock. It took six years of perseverance and hard work. His hope for freedom kept him alive, and he finally achieved his dream, escaping to a beach in Mexico.

I scratched through my last napkin note, "Take Action," and wrote instead "Get Busy Living or Get Busy Dying." And so I say to you right here, right now: The choice is yours to make—get busy living or get busy dying.

CHAPTER 3

Pursue Your Passion, Success Does Not Equal Money

IN HAWAII, CLARENCE WENT OFF TO HIS CONVENTION, AND I FOUND the waves I was seeking. But, true to form, I did more than just surf. I began to work on the book you're now reading.

Okay, wc all agree that you want to be really successful. The absolute first thing you must do is to find out what you are good at. Usually, if you are good at something, you enjoy doing it; you might even love it and be passionate about it. The key to success is finding out what you are passionate about, and pursuing it. It sounds so easy but many people pursue a career because their parents or other people pressured them to do something to secure a living. Often, these people find themselves doing something they dislike, or even worse, hate.

Have you discovered what you are passionate about or capable of excelling at? If not, this chapter will help you identify what it is you should be doing, whether you're still in school, have been working for some years and are contemplating a mid-career change, or you're retired. Once you understand yourself and find your true potential, you will achieve the kind of success that only comes from being happy and passionate about your work. Virtually all successful people are not only good at what they do, but they also love doing what they do. It's the one-two combination of success: finding out what you are good at is the jab, loving it is the uppercut. Then, you're on your way to a knockout career.

In order for you to figure out your strongest skills, you should take the two tests described below and in the Appendix. It is essential that you understand there are no right or wrong answers. The whole process will help you discover more about who you are, given your personality, talents, and preferences. After completing these two tests, you will better understand how you tend to react, function and behave in almost any setting. Once again remember: there are no right or wrong answers. The results are a reflection of your talents, likes and dislikes, which you may not even realize.

Who Are You?

Everyone can observe a great variety of personality traits among people. For example, some people are very outgoing and extraverted, while other people are more quiet and introspective. Therefore, it's easy to see that everybody is gifted with a unique personality.

One of the ways you can easily and quickly begin to discover character traits about yourself, and ways in which you can begin to improve certain aspects of yourself is to complete a popular online self-examination quiz.

Emode's Ultimate Personality Test

www.emode.com is the undisputed leader in online self-assessment testing with more than sixty million tests saved in its data warehouse including 1.6 billion test answers. More than 100 assessment tests on the website may be perused for free, but users of the site have the option to purchase a 10–15 page comprehensive analysis of their individual test results. In fact, Emode has been so successful since being founded in 1999, that the company was honored in 2002 with a "Webby Award" in the prestigious Rising Star category, recognizing Emode as the fastest growing website of 2002. The Webby Awards are the Academy Awards of the Internet, and the leading international honor for achievement online. The Rising Star Award is based on percent growth of visitors in 2002, as measured by Nielsen/NetRatings.

Research has shown that people whose personalities are well-suited to their job environments are happier and more successful. Wouldn't it be great if you can actually "figure out" your personality? Well, you can!

While the human personality is is far too complex to categorize there are general "personality types" that can be identified. One of the advantages of defining these types is that once you know how someone tends to behave, you can start to predict future behavior.

History of Personality Tests

As early as the fifth century B.C., the Greek philosopher/physician Hippocrates recorded the first known personality model. He based his four "types" on the amount of body fluids an individual possessed. The Greek physician Galen expounded upon Hippocrates' theory. He believed a predominance of blood led to a confident person who was cheerful and strong. A predominance of mucus led to an indifferent, slow personality. A predominance of black bile led to a depressed personality, and a predominance of yellow bile led to a violent and strong personality.

German philosopher Immanuel Kant later popularized these ideas in the 1700's, when he organized those constructs along two axes, feelings and activity. Depression represented weak feelings, confidence reflected strong feelings. Indifference represented weak activity, violence represented strong activity.

The notion of four basic temperaments eventually became the basis of a number of late 19th–20th-century behavioral theories. Some of the most significant work on this subject was done by the Swiss psychoanalyst, Carl G. Jung. In 1922, he introduced four categories of mental functioning: sensing, intuition, thinking and feeling in his work. At the time, Jung's ideas about personality types went largely unnoticed, due to the frenzy surrounding the modern psychoanalytic theories of Sigmund Freud, B.F. Skinner and others.

In the 1950s, however, Isabel Myers and her daughter Katherine Briggs revived Jung's ideas. Myers and Briggs used Jung's personality types as a base and then devised a 16-type indicator designed to identify patterns of human action. This test became the Myers-Briggs Type Indicator (MBTI), a tool for identifying different aspects of someone's personality. This "tool" exposed a whole new international audience to Jung's psychological types. More than three million Myers-Briggs Type Indicator tests are administered each year in the U.S.

Modern Personality Tests

In addition to the MBTI, which is still one of the most widely used personality tests, other popular theories and tests exist. The Keirsey Temperament Sorter is a test built around David Keirsey's groundbreaking 1978 book *Please Understand Me*. The Keirsey Temperament Sorter is similar to the MBTI in its use of four dimensions and 16 categories, but the Keirsey method claims to have a more complex system of characterization.

Although they are not perfect, personality tests can help you understand and better relate to yourself and the world. They can also help you understand why you are the way you are. You can also use them to understand other people, not only to improve friendships, but to facilitate work relationships and career choices.

The Science Behind Emode's Ultimate Personality Test

Emode and a team of four Personality Test PhDs wanted to create a test that was not only fun but also grounded in scientific basis.

The Ultimate Personality Test in the Appendix at the end of this chapter consists of 50 questions distilled from extensive research that tested thousands of qualities associated with personality.

The Ultimate Personality Test accurately measures what many psychologists consider to be the central components and fundamental dimensions of personality. The results will tell you what your personality type is and how your personality type reacts to a wide range of situations.

Emode's complete Ultimate Personality Test is found in the Appendix at the end of this chapter. You should take the test. When you're finished, you should log on to the Emode website. The cost to take the test on the site is $14.95. When you complete it, you will receive almost instantly a 10–15 page report with specific information about your personality type. The Emode site has literally hundreds of tests, most of them similar in length, but all of which you learn the results instantly. As a kicker, when you sign up for just one test, Emode offers test-takers free access to the site for one week, which means you can take as many tests as you choose and also receive the results.

The important thing to remember is that the scores from all of your tests are an indication of where you stand today. Everyone possesses the capacity to improve and change. To help you do just that, when you receive the completed report when taking the test online, Emode's experts provide a series of action steps in each section intended to help you fulfill your potential.

I Took the Test, It Changed My Life

Years ago, I took the Myers Briggs Type Indicator (MBTI) test. Reading the details of this extensive report at that time helped me think about my career and had a significant impact on my future. It was July 1994 and I had just graduated from Columbia Law School. Although I was about to begin my new legal career, something felt wrong.

If my accomplishments in law school were an indicator of future achievement, by all accounts I had a promising legal career ahead of me that would begin with a clerkship for a federal judge in the Southern District of Florida. My bags were packed, and in two weeks I was ready to move with my wife and two-month-old daughter from New York City to Miami. But at the last minute, with no idea how I would repay the $70,000 in law school loans that I now owed, I changed my mind. Although I was excited about embarking on this new opportunity, something about it did not feel right.

Everyone was happy for me, my parents were ecstatic, my wife was thrilled, but despite all the excitement on the surface, I had mixed feelings. So far I had proved to myself that I had the skills to be a good lawyer. But the passion was still missing. I reflected on the Myers-Briggs assessment, and I thought about the times I was happiest such as meeting the challenges of exploring my leadership skills while at the U.S. Air Force Academy. I also thought about the entrepreneurial small businesses that I started while in law school and how much I enjoyed those experiences.

After reviewing all this in my mind, and reflecting on my MBTI assessment, it occurred to me that my strengths, my happiness, and my successes to date were centered on leadership and entrepreneurial businesses, and these aspects of my personality did not translate into a career in the legal profession. Could I have been a good lawyer? Maybe. Nevertheless, in my mind being a good lawyer and being a successful lawyer are two different things. And therein lies the difference. I don't think I would ever be passionate about practicing law. It did not inherently call for me to draw upon the traits that I knew I possessed and the skills I enjoyed using. The MBTI was proof positive that I had to follow my gut instincts and pull the plug on the judicial clerkship.

The Law Is Out, Business Is In

I chose to go into business. When I shared my decision with my family, my father-in-law Seymour Holtzman suggested that if I wanted to go into business, I should apprentice with him for a few years, just as I had intended to clerk for the federal judge. Seymour, a brilliant, self-made businessman, was someone from whom I could learn a great deal. He had built and operated a number of successful businesses including several well-known public companies. If I ever thought about going into business for myself, I could not have dreamed up a better opportunity.

Here is a perfect example of the importance of how our lives can take a turn when we make decisions based upon important knowledge of our own personalities and strengths. If I had not made a decision to pursue a business career, the opportunity to apprentice with my father-in-law would never have arisen. I would not have gone on to found Sterling Financial Group of Companies, and most likely, I would not be writing this book.

Discovering Your Strengths

The second test I urge you to take is the brainchild of Marcus Buckingham and Donald O. Clifton, who coauthored the national bestseller *Now, Discover Your Strengths,* that presents a revolutionary program to help you identify your talents, build them into strengths, and enjoy consistent success.[1] At Sterling Financial, we took these revolutionary ideas, applied them, and completely changed our corporate culture, after which our company took off almost immediately. Their book and the resulting test are the product of a 25-year, multimillion-dollar effort by the Gallup Organization, based on over two million psychological profiles of people all over the world in various professions. After interviewing many successful people, the authors identified the type of personality traits that were predominant in certain individuals and certain careers, and developed an index to help people like you and me uncover and analyze our strengths.

Unfortunately, in school and at our workplace, most people are encouraged to find, analyze, and correct our weaknesses to become successful. Clifton and Buckingham believe this advice is well intended but misguided. To excel in a chosen field, you need to develop your strengths, not your weaknesses. I can remember back in junior high school when I brought home five A's and a D in geometry, and I spent the next six months killing myself to become a mediocre geometry student. Whereas athletes like Tiger Woods and Michael Jordan spent all their efforts finding, practicing, and refining their strengths, which resulted in their becoming superstars.

If you believe these concepts, then, you'll need to suspend any interest you might have in your weaknesses and instead focus on your strengths. When you buy *Now, Discover Your Strengths* you will find a unique identification number on the back of the dust jacket cover that allows you to access the authors' Website at www.strengthsfinder.com. After completing a web-based interview that takes about 45 minutes, you'll discover your five most prominent strengths. Once you know which of the 34 strengths—such as Discipline, Activator, Empathy, Restorative, or Self-Assurance—you lead with, the book will show you how to leverage them for powerful results at three levels: your own personal development, your success as a manager, and the success of your organization. For example, it was discovered that 95 percent of doctors had the Restorative strength in their top five, because they like to fix things. When I took the test, I discovered my five signature strengths were Competition, Achiever, Activator, Strategic, and Focus.

Not only do the results of this test provide a detailed analysis of your own strengths, but it also analyzes how you should manage someone with each of the 34 different strengths. What we found at our company was that many people were performing functions that they were simply not good at, based on their innate strengths. This fact was consistent with the finding of The Gallup Organization research.

The Gallup scientists asked the following question of more than 1.7 million employees in 101 companies from 63 countries: "At work do you have the opportunity to do what you do best every day?" A pitiful 20 percent of people strongly agreed that they had an opportunity to do what they did best every day. The most counterintuitive fact was that the higher someone climbed on the corporate ladder, the less likely that person would be playing to his or her strengths. When I realized that most organizations were operating at only 20 percent capacity, I saw this as a tremendous opportunity. If I could get 60 percent of my employees to use their strengths every day, I could triple the productivity of the company.

Based largely on these findings, we completely changed the assumptions we had about our employees. The most important asset of our company became our people. Instead of assuming that anyone could be trained to become competent in any position, we analyzed each person's unique talents. We felt an employee's greatest growth would naturally come from the area of that person's greatest strengths. We quickly discovered that the majority of our employees and senior managers were miscast, and we had to rebuild the company by playing to each person's strengths.

You too can use the results of Emode's Ultimate Personality Test as well as the StrengthFinder Profile discussed in *Now Discover Your Strengths* to zero in on your innate talents and achieve success.

The Ultimate Personality Test

Know the Real You

1. I'm more romantic than most people I know.
   - ❑ Strongly agree
   - ☑ Agree
   - ❑ Disagree
   - ❑ Strongly disagree

2. I set ambitious goals for myself, and I work hard to achieve them.
   - ❑ Strongly agree
   - ☑ Agree
   - ❑ Disagree
   - ❑ Strongly disagree

3. I get very upset if I catch my partner checking out other people.
   - ❑ Strongly agree
   - ☑ Agree
   - ❑ Disagree
   - ❑ Strongly disagree

4. I like situations that need some real thinking.
   - ❑ Strongly agree
   - ☑ Agree
   - ❑ Disagree
   - ❑ Strongly disagree

5. Overall, I think the government is doing a good job.
   - ❑ Strongly agree
   - ❑ Agree
   - ❑ Disagree
   - ☑ Strongly disagree

6. I have lots of energy.
   - ☑ Strongly agree
   - ❑ Agree
   - ❑ Disagree
   - ❑ Strongly disagree

7. I'm happiest when I'm with my friends.
   - ☑ Strongly agree
   - ❑ Agree
   - ❑ Disagree
   - ❑ Strongly disagree

8. My attractiveness to other people is very important to me.
   - ❑ Strongly agree
   - ☑ Agree
   - ❑ Disagree
   - ❑ Strongly disagree

9. I keep in close touch with my friends and family.
   - ❑ Strongly agree
   - ☑ Agree
   - ❑ Disagree
   - ❑ Strongly disagree

10. I have a positive attitude about myself.
    - ❑ Strongly agree
    - ❑ Agree
    - ☑ Disagree
    - ❑ Strongly disagree

11. Sex is best when two people are in love.
    - ☐ Strongly agree
    - ☑ Agree
    - ☐ Disagree
    - ☐ Strongly disagree

12. I tend to blow off my duties.
    - ☑ Strongly agree
    - ☐ Agree
    - ☐ Disagree
    - ☐ Strongly disagree

13. My relationships with other people are very important to me.
    - ☑ Strongly agree
    - ☐ Agree
    - ☐ Disagree
    - ☐ Strongly disagree

14. I'll pick my nose in public if I think no one's looking.
    - ☐ Strongly agree
    - ☐ Agree
    - ☑ Disagree
    - ☐ Strongly disagree

15. I like the exhilaration of unpredictable situations.
    - ☐ Strongly agree
    - ☐ Agree
    - ☑ Disagree
    - ☐ Strongly disagree

16. My job always takes a back seat to my personal life.
    - ☐ Strongly agree
    - ☑ Agree
    - ☐ Disagree
    - ☐ Strongly disagree

17. A consistent routine lets me enjoy life more.
    - ❏ Strongly agree
    - ❏ Agree
    - ☑ Disagree
    - ❏ Strongly disagree

18. I often put up a front to keep others from knowing the real me.
    - ☑ Strongly agree
    - ❏ Agree
    - ❏ Disagree
    - ❏ Strongly disagree

19. I'm a kind person.
    - ❏ Strongly agree
    - ☑ Agree
    - ❏ Disagree
    - ❏ Strongly disagree

20. Loud noises or chaotic scenes really bother me.
    - ❏ Strongly agree
    - ❏ Agree
    - ❏ Disagree
    - ☑ Strongly disagree

21. I admire people who own expensive things.
    - ❏ Strongly agree
    - ❏ Agree
    - ☑ Disagree
    - ❏ Strongly disagree

22. I like most of the people I meet.
    - ❏ Strongly agree
    - ☑ Agree
    - ❏ Disagree
    - ❏ Strongly disagree

23. It's important for me to always look good.
    - ❏ Strongly agree
    - ❏ Agree
    - ☑ Disagree
    - ❏ Strongly disagree

24. I can be a jealous person.
    - ❏ Strongly agree
    - ☑ Agree
    - ❏ Disagree
    - ❏ Strongly disagree

25. I have an opinion on everything.
    - ☑ Strongly agree
    - ❏ Agree
    - ❏ Disagree
    - ❏ Strongly disagree

26. People look at me as a pretty spontaneous person.
    - ☑ Strongly agree
    - ❏ Agree
    - ❏ Disagree
    - ❏ Strongly disagree

27. My possessions speak toward my success in life.
    - ❏ Strongly agree
    - ❏ Agree
    - ☑ Disagree
    - ❏ Strongly disagree

28. I like intellectual conversations.
    - ❏ Strongly agree
    - ❏ Agree
    - ☑ Disagree
    - ❏ Strongly disagree

29. I'm a tense person.
    - ❒ Strongly agree
    - ☑ Agree
    - ❒ Disagree
    - ❒ Strongly disagree

30. I like who I am.
    - ❒ Strongly agree
    - ❒ Agree
    - ☑ Disagree
    - ❒ Strongly disagree

31. I hate to be with unpredictable people.
    - ❒ Strongly agree
    - ❒ Agree
    - ❒ Disagree
    - ☑ Strongly disagree

32. I'd describe myself as a pretty soft-hearted person.
    - ❒ Strongly agree
    - ☑ Agree
    - ❒ Disagree
    - ❒ Strongly disagree

33. I like dealing with new and unusual situations.
    - ❒ Strongly agree
    - ❒ Agree
    - ☑ Disagree
    - ❒ Strongly disagree

34. My life revolves around the people I'm close to.
    - ❒ Strongly agree
    - ☑ Agree
    - ☑ Disagree
    - ❒ Strongly disagree

35. If I could afford more things, I'd probably be happier.
   - ❏ Strongly agree
   - ☑ Agree
   - ❏ Disagree
   - ❏ Strongly disagree

36. It bothers me when too much is going on around me.
   - ❏ Strongly agree
   - ☑ Agree
   - ☑ Disagree
   - ❏ Strongly disagree

37. I get a warm feeling from cooperating with others.
   - ❏ Strongly agree
   - ❏ Agree
   - ☑ Disagree
   - ❏ Strongly disagree

38. I thrive on competition.
   - ☑ Strongly agree
   - ❏ Agree
   - ❏ Disagree
   - ❏ Strongly disagree

39. I communicate well with loved ones.
   - ☑ Strongly agree
   - ❏ Agree
   - ❏ Disagree
   - ❏ Strongly disagree

40. I'm a worrier.
   - ❏ Strongly agree
   - ☑ Agree
   - ❏ Disagree
   - ❏ Strongly disagree

41. I like to do things on the spur of the moment.
    - ☑ Strongly agree
    - ❐ Agree
    - ❐ Disagree
    - ❐ Strongly disagree

42. It's important to me that I'm more successful than my friends.
    - ❐ Strongly agree
    - ☑ Agree
    - ❐ Disagree
    - ❐ Strongly disagree

43. I'm a big time-waster.
    - ☑ Strongly agree
    - ❐ Agree
    - ❐ Disagree
    - ❐ Strongly disagree

44. Abstract thinking doesn't appeal to me.
    - ❐ Strongly agree
    - ❐ Agree
    - ❐ Disagree
    - ☑ Strongly disagree

45. It's more important to me to get ahead than get along.
    - ❐ Strongly agree
    - ☑ Agree
    - ❐ Disagree
    - ❐ Strongly disagree

46. Overall, I'm satisfied with myself.
    - ❐ Strongly agree
    - ☑ Agree
    - ❐ Disagree
    - ❐ Strongly disagree

47. I like owning things that make a good impression on others.
    - ☐ Strongly agree
    - ☑ Agree
    - ☐ Disagree
    - ☐ Strongly disagree

48. I'll work 24/7 if that's what it takes for a successful career.
    - ☐ Strongly agree
    - ☐ Agree
    - ☑ Disagree
    - ☐ Strongly disagree

49. I feel pretty useless sometimes.
    - ☑ Strongly agree
    - ☐ Agree
    - ☐ Disagree
    - ☐ Strongly disagree

50. I want my life to be filled with intellectual challenges.
    - ☐ Strongly agree
    - ☐ Agree
    - ☐ Disagree
    - ☑ Strongly disagree

PART TWO

TURN YOUR BELIEFS INTO SUCCESS MAGNETS

CHAPTER 4

Olivia's Magic Bracelet

THE POWER OF THE MIND CAN BE SEEN MOST CLEARLY WHEN EXAMINING the results of placebo studies. The "placebo effect" is how doctors describe the phenomenon in which patients get better because they expect the treatment to work, even though they're actually given a sugar pill that looks like the real medication. One explanation for the placebo effect is that confidence in the treatment results in a mind-over-body effect. Evidently, when patients take this sugar pill, they believe they are going to get well because the doctor told them it would make them better. Ultimately, the person does become well. Patients don't just think they're getting better. Objective test results demonstrate that they actually are better.

The Magic Bracelet

There was a brief period when my daughter was having trouble making friends at school. One night, after dinner, I took her into my study and we sat on my couch. "Olivia," I said, as she looked curiously into my eyes, not knowing what to expect from me. "I know you've been having some trouble making friends at school lately, and I think I have just the thing that can help you."

"Really, Dad?" she said with a tone of hope in her voice.

I reached into my pocket and took out a little box. I looked at her, she looked at me, and I could tell she was puzzled. "Here, Olivia, this is for you."

She took the box and opened it. "Wow, Dad, thanks," she said, gleefully, as she removed a delicate silver charm bracelet. "Dad," she said looking up at me after reviewing her new gift, "how can this help me?"

"Olivia," I said, as I opened it and motioned for her arm. I repeated her name for effect as I began to clasp it on her wrist. "Olivia, the only way this bracelet works is when you meet people and introduce yourself, you must look them directly in the eyes and in those first few moments think to yourself, 'I love you.'"

"Okay, Daddy," she said, "I'll try it tomorrow and let you know how it goes. Can I wear the bracelet to bed tonight?" she asked. "Of course," I said. I got a great big hug, and she was off to show the new bracelet to her Mom.

The next day after I got home from work, Olivia came running up to me after I entered the house. "Daddy, Daddy," she said, as I leaned down to pick her up.

"What, Sweet Pea?" I said, not sure if the bracelet worked, or if something else might come out of her mouth. One thing you learn as a parent is that you never ever know what a child is going to say. "I said hello to two girls and a boy today that I thought didn't really like me before!"

"Really?" I said, "that's wonderful."

"Yeah, we're friends now."

"That's terrific," I said. "So the bracelet worked, huh?"

"Uh huh," she said, as I carried her and walked through the house to the kitchen to see my wife.

"Honey, did you hear that Olivia made three new friends today," I said to Allison as I entered the kitchen, put down Olivia, and kissed my wife hello.

"Can I wear the bracelet to school tomorrow?" Olivia asked.

"Yes," I said, but I also told her that the bracelet only worked for two days and that after tomorrow the magic would be gone from the bracelet and be in her. Olivia looked at me with eyes wide open. "Really, in me?" she asked. Olivia came home the next day and the scene was almost exactly the same. She had made two more friends. When I took the bracelet back from her, I told her that I had to give it back to the man who had given it to me so that he could give it to other little children who also needed the magic to help them.

The Magic's in You!

Olivia thought that there was magic in the bracelet; it changed her life. It gave her the confidence that she needed to be able to talk to other kids and make new friends. Now that she knew she had the magic inside herself, she would have confidence all the time.

The magic you'll find in this next story is not found in any bracelet. It can be found in paper and pen when you write down your dreams and activate the power of your subconscious mind. It is the story of a man I met through work on the advisory board of the school that my daughter Olivia attends.

The "Rocky" of Medicine

"Ever since I could remember, I wanted to be a star," says Charles D. Kelman, who came upon this idea at the tender age of 4 when his first offhand original quip caught the attention of a room full of adults. It made them happy, it made him happy, and he loved this feeling.

While just a youngster, this craving for center stage led him to perform as a singer, a saxophonist, and a comedian. Kelman became such a good entertainer that one night his father asked him to perform for him. At the age of 16, after 10 years of saxophone lessons and 14,600 hours of practice in the basement, Kelman put on a command performance upstairs in the family's living room. At the conclusion of the song, Kelman's father asked, "Do you play that better than Jimmy Dorsey?"

The young Kelman replied that to the best of his knowledge, Jimmy Dorsey did not play that song. After thinking about it, he confessed that if Dorsey did, he would probably play it better.

With that, Kelman's father made a remark that would change the boy's life and set in motion a set of circumstances that would literally change the medical world.

The young Kelman was creative, artistic and inventive, and his father knew this about his son. He knew that he was talented and that his talents should be directed to serve others. Kelman's father believed that his son could truly make a contribution to the world, perhaps in music and other endeavors where the young man might focus his attention. But perhaps he could do something truly great. "Son," said father Kelman benignly, "It's your life. You can do with it whatever you like. You can be a songwriter, a singer, a saxophone player, or any other thing, but first you'll be a doctor."

According to Kelman, there was no discussion about it. "In those days you did what your father told you." Unfortunately, his high school principal told him he wasn't college material and ought to go to trade school instead. In fact, when Kelman told him he was going to be a surgeon, the principal started laughing hysterically. But even without his principal's recommendation, Kelman went to college and soon thereafter studied to become a doctor at the University of Geneva in Switzerland, all the while dreaming of being a musician, a songwriter, or an entertainer. While attending medical school, Kelman found time to play his saxophone in bars and nightclubs. He kept his dream alive while abiding by his father's wishes. While studying abroad, Kelman doubled by day as a medical student and by night as a musician, cruising bars, looking for music gigs, meeting people, and forming relationships with other musicians.

As the time went by, Kelman was torn. Although he excelled in his studies, he also excelled at his musical exploits. He was always thinking about whether to be a doctor or a musician or an entertainer.

Kelman graduated from medical school and returned to the United States to pursue his medical career, but his passion for playing the saxophone remained. Ultimately, music served as a thread that weaved through the fabric of his life, a significant factor influencing his decision to become an ophthalmic physician and eye surgeon. Says Kelman, reflecting on his career, "For the first 10 years I'm not sure if I was a musician playing a doctor or a doctor playing an instrument."

One of the keys to Dr. Kelman's success was the clear articulation of his goals and his extraordinary perseverance. In fact, Kelman says that his life changed when he was given a little book called *It Works*.[1] Although the author is unknown, the book has more than 1 million copies in print. The entire book, all 28 pages, explains the critical importance of writing down your life's dreams, reviewing them at least three times a day, and discussing them with no one.

Kelman followed these principles and wrote down 40 goals on his list. In order to focus on what was really important to him, he winnowed his list to 10 of his most important dreams. He explains, "When you know exactly what you want and focus on it three times a day, the power of your subconscious mind takes over and it leads you to achieve your goals regardless of how grand they may be." Kelman is a perfect example. "I achieved every single thing I wanted to." Some of his original goals: international recognition for a major breakthrough in the medical field; to be happily married with children; to make a groundbreaking contribution to society; to be in excellent physical health; to continue to have fun and be successful with his music; to own and pilot his own helicopter; to be financially secure; and to have children with whom he could have a close relationship. Like Sylvester Stallone's character in the movie *Rocky*, this daily focus on his dreams helped forge an unbreakable human spirit, with astonishing perseverance.

In 1962, after following the principles of the book for just two years, Dr. Kelman devised the cryoprobe, a freezing instrument for the extraction of cataracts within their capsules. This procedure became the most widely used method for cataract removal in the world until 1978, when he introduced a new technique which still remains the most widely used method of cataract surgery. He won numerous awards for his medical successes, including the American Achievement Award, whose previous recipients include Dr. Jonas Salk, who developed the polio vaccine, and Dr. Michael DeBakey, known as the father of modern cardiovascular surgery. Kelman was also awarded the Inventor of the Year Award from the New York Patent, Trademark and Copyright Law Association for his development of the Kelman phacoemulsification procedure, and he was awarded the prestigious National Medal of Technology by President George H. Bush, and numerous other awards in the medical field. Kelman's autobiography *Through My Eyes* is a fascinating story that shows how focus and perseverance pay off.[3]

Kelman's father's early assessments of his son's talents were realized. He achieved worldwide acclaim as an innovator, creative thinker, and inventor with over 150 patents to his name. However, never once did Dr. Kelman give up on his dream to pursue his passion for music, entertainment, and show business.

Following the secrets he learned in his little book, which now he gives out to all his friends, he went on to record music professionally, performed at Carnegie Hall, and entertained on many television programs including *The Tonight Show, The David Letterman Show* and *Oprah*. Still, Kelman says, "First, I am a doctor." His mother and father would be proud.

Program Your Success Compass Today!

Dr. Kelman's extraordinary success exemplifies the power of writing down and visualizing your dreams daily. So now it's your turn! I have developed a web-based software program—*Success Compass*™—that stimulates you to dream about everything you would like to accomplish in your lifetime. Right now you can literally change your life by using the *Success Compass*™, available free on-line at *www.successcompass.com*. Once on-line, a special wizard asks you questions and gives examples in a dozen key areas of your life, from advancing your career, to improving your relationships, to getting healthy and fit, to achieving financial security, and many more.

Once you list your dreams and goals, next you prioritize them into the ten most important ones. You can then print them out or request an e-mail reminder three times a day or even order a laminated, wallet-sized version. As Dr. Kelman observed, "to activate your subconscious mind you need to focus on your dreams three times a day." By having your *Success Compass*™ handy at all times, you can make it an integral part of your daily actions.

If you knew that you could make a decision today that would literally change your life for the better—would you do it? I urge you to take thirty minutes today and sit down and complete your *Success Compass*™. You will be amazed at the power of this simple step to crystallize your dreams into writing. Once you do it, and you look at your list three times a day, the energy of your subconscious mind will begin to move you towards those dreams.

The next part of the book will teach you 14 "success beliefs" that I have seen work for nearly every accomplished person I know. If you apply these success magnets to your personal life, I am confident that you can succeed wherever your *Success Compass*™ takes you.

CHAPTER 5

Success Belief 1:
Follow the Initiative
of Lieutenant Rowan

DURING MY CHILDHOOD IN PANAMA, ONE OF MY FAVORITE SHORT stories was *A Message to Garcia*[1] because my last name was in the title and, more importantly, the story taught me a lesson about initiative.

A Message to Garcia was written over 100 years ago by Elbert Hubbard as a filler for a small magazine called *The Philistine*. Orders came in for over a million copies of the magazine, because people wanted to read the article. Since being published, the story has been read by an estimated 45 million people throughout the world. The short story still enjoys widespread popularity, and not just in the Charles Garcia family. Leaders all over the world use the book to inspire their employees. Governor Jeb Bush of Florida has made the booklet required reading for his staff. I think the story should be read by employees of every company and government agency.

Let Nothing Stand in Your Way

With the United States on the brink of war with Spain in 1899, President McKinley desperately needed information about the strength of the Spanish troops from the leader of the insurgent forces in Cuba, General Garcia. However, General Garcia could not be reached by telegraph or mail because he was deep in the jungles of Cuba. Lieutenant Andrew Summers Rowan was dispatched with the letter from the president, which was sealed in an oilskin pouch and strapped across his chest.

Rowan's first stop was in Jamaica where he met with Cuban exiles. While there, he risked arrest by the authorities and was led through hostile territory by Gervacio Sabio, a man exiled from Cuba for disagreeing with the rule of Spain. Sabio had lost his thumb as punishment for resisting Spanish rule in Cuba.

From Jamaica, Rowan left for Cuba aboard a small fishing boat. The 100-mile-journey north was perilous because of the Spanish "lanchas," light boats carrying heavily armed Spanish troops. Rowan, on the other hand, was armed only with a Smith & Wesson revolver and a rifle that could fire a single round at a time, if he was lucky. Any run-ins with the "lanchas" would mean sure defeat for Rowan and the end of his mission. After anchoring in the darkness for a night, 50 yards from the shore of Cuba, Rowan and his men started off through the jungles in search of General Garcia. Through rough terrain and risking capture, the mission finally reached Bayamo, General Garcia's headquarters, where his arrival was met with cheers from the General's army. Once the message was delivered, he now had to take General Garcia's answer back to President McKinley!

Rowan's return trip was equally perilous. Through the treacherous waters, Rowan and his men sailed, bailed, and broiled in the hot sun to complete Rowan's mission. After being quarantined temporarily for a suspected case of yellow fever, Rowan finally completed the last leg of his dangerous assignment. He arrived in Washington with the crucial information for the president. Rowan had done his duty, though he didn't see it as heroic.

Hubbard lauded Rowan's extraordinary achievement in *A Message to Garcia*. According to Hubbard, the world needs more people like Rowan, who do the job without making excuses for not getting it done. Once told what is to be done, such men and women find a way to do it.

A Message from General Galvin to Garcia

Many years had passed since my father gave me his copy of *A Message to Garcia* and we read it together. After graduating from the United States Air Force Academy, I entered the Air Force. At age 24, I became special assistant to General John R. Galvin, who later was named Supreme Allied Commander of the North Atlantic Treaty Organization (NATO). I worked for General Galvin for several years while he was commander of the United States Southern Command in the Republic of Panama.

When General Galvin gave me my first assignment, I nervously came back to him a few hours later with a lot of questions. The general snapped at me, "Lieutenant. How many stars do you have on your shoulder?"

"None, sir," I said, hoping my voice wouldn't crack.

"And how many stars do I have on mine?"

"Four, sir," I answered.

"Lieutenant," General Galvin snarled, "If you want me to do your job, then what do I need you for?" With that rhetorical question, I was dismissed. I was sure my military career was over.

Before I left, the General gave me a piece of advice that I never forgot. "Garcia," he called out to me. "Yes, sir," I said, spinning around immediately.

"Don't bring me problems, bring me solutions." I exited the room wondering which part of the world I would be reassigned to tomorrow.

Later, when I finally did bring my proposed solution to General Galvin, he wasn't satisfied, although this encounter was less traumatic. The General explained that I needed to bring him at least three solutions and tell him why I picked one over the other two. He said, "If you always think of at least three different ways to solve a problem, you will look at things from a different perspective and you'll make sure that you are not grasping at the first solution that comes to mind." Instead of following the example of Lieutenant Rowan, I had asked dumb questions rather than figuring out solutions for myself.

Successful People Bring Solutions to the Table

A great leader is a problem solver, but everyone in the company should offer solutions and fix problems. I expect managers to fix problems within 24 hours. Any problems that hang around more than a day go on my "watch list." You should look to hire problem solvers, not people who point out problems. Finding out what your problems are isn't difficult. Finding solutions is. Brian Tracy, the author of *Focal Point*, says the key to becoming an excellent problem solver is to focus on possible solutions to every dilemma. Instead of getting angry or blaming others when something goes wrong, Tracy recommends asking yourself, "What's the solution?" and "What's the next step?" Tracy writes, "A truly effective person is one who has developed a wonderful ability to respond constructively to the inevitable problems and difficulties of day-to-day life."[2]

What kind of employee are you? Do you run to your boss to whine about why you couldn't finish an assignment or do you get the job done in spite of the obstacles in your path? Are you a Lieutenant Rowan or someone who is extremely good at pointing out why you can't do something? Are you an employee who is willing to plow through the jungle to complete your mission or would you have given up when vines and brush blocked the trail? If you run your own business, do you follow the clear and unobstructed path or do you blaze a trail through difficult terrain? Do you blame the economy and the government for problems or do you seize new opportunities that others shy away from? Do you go forward fearlessly or sit back while others lead the way?

In his book, *E-Leader: Reinventing Leadership in a Connected Economy*, Robert Hargrove distinguishes between the CEO who is a steward and the CEO who is an entrepreneur. The steward polishes grandma's silver and protects the past. The entrepreneur creates something new that never existed before.[3]

Bring Solutions to Your Personal Life

In your personal life, you probably know many people who are content to talk about their problems without looking to solve them. Even when you offer suggestions, they dismiss them and tell you why those solutions don't work. Sadly, these people continue to fail because they dwell on their problems instead of seeking solutions.

It's your decision. You can choose to show initiative in every endeavor, regardless of the obstacles that get in the way. You can solve problems and watch them dissolve, or you can allow your dreams to dissolve in the face of problems. More than 100 years after President McKinley sent his message to Garcia, former president Ronald Reagan sent his own message to the American people. As Reagan said, "If we make up our mind on what we are going to make of our lives, then work hard toward that goal, we never lose—somehow we win out."[4]

At the end of this chapter you'll find the first of many messages *from Garcia to you.* They are offered to pay tribute to Hubbard's book and to summarize the key points in every chapter. If you take them to heart, these messages can help you find success.

Take Responsibility and Make No Excuses

When you're a first-year cadet at the Air Force Academy, you spend considerable time getting chewed out by upperclassmen. As you stand at attention, you are only allowed to utter one of four appropriate responses: "Yes, Sir"; "No, Sir"; "I don't understand, Sir"; or "No excuse, Sir."

If you're a teacher, you've probably heard every excuse in the book from children who didn't do their homework. It's bad enough when children make excuses, but hearing them from adults is worse. Every day managers hear employees say they're too busy to finish an assignment or they didn't get the data from another department. Whether you're 5 or 55, excuses are a way to shift responsibility from yourself to someone else. Successful people take responsibility rather than shifting it to another person or department.

If you find yourself being nagged by others, take a look at yourself and see if you might be failing to follow through on your commitments. If you aren't performing well, take responsibility for your actions and make improvements instead of making excuses. If you're genuinely overloaded, then you should work on becoming more organized. Work and problems start to mount when you're not proactive. As President John F. Kennedy said, "The best time to repair the roof is when the sun is shining."

A Message from Garcia

Show initiative. Be creative. Be resourceful and imaginative in executing your duties and completing projects. Take responsibility for your actions and don't make excuses for not being able to complete them. Are you a Lieutenant Rowan, or are you a Corporal Complainer? Do you focus on the obstacles that stand in your way or do you look for ways to get the job done? How much time do you spend complaining about an assignment instead of just doing it?

You should devise at least three solutions to any serious problem. This process forces you to think of various solutions. By weighing the pros and cons of every conceivable idea, you can solve your problem in the most efficient way.

CHAPTER 6

Success Belief 2: You Need *Ganas*

YOU NEED MORE THAN A BOOK TO HELP YOU SUCCEED. YOU NEED what my friend Jaime Escalante calls *ganas*, the Spanish word for desire. Having goals is not enough. You must have the burning desire within your heart to achieve your goals.

Escalante, a physics and math teacher in Bolivia, migrated to the United States in 1964. He spoke no English and obviously lacked the necessary credentials to continue teaching. After settling in California, he worked all day as a busboy in a restaurant and then took courses at night at Pasadena City College. He graduated from Cal State in Los Angeles with a B.A. in math and electronics in 1974. Escalante took a teaching job at Garfield High School in East Los Angeles. He was supposed to teach computer science, but his students were lacking basic math skills. Nevertheless, in an environment of gangs, drugs, and violence, Escalante taught advanced placement (AP) calculus—a college-level course for advanced high school students—to a small group of students. (Escalante's efforts at Garfield High were turned into an award-winning movie, *Stand and Deliver*, in which Edward James Olmos played the part of Escalante.) In 1982, the students took the advanced placement calculus exam and passed.

Jaime Escalante's students could have made excuses when the Educational Testing Service (ETS) invalidated their test scores in

1982 after they passed the AP exam. The ETS accused Escalante's students of cheating and invalidated their test scores simply because they believed that these poor, minority Hispanic students from the barrio could not possibly have done so well, especially so many of them. Even though the students hadn't studied for months and were out of school, 12 agreed to retake the test. Every one of them passed the exam.[1]

In the ensuing years, Escalante's calculus program grew phenomenally. In 1983 both enrollment in his class and the number of students passing the AP calculus test more than doubled, with 33 taking the exam and 30 passing it. In 1987, 73 passed the test, and another 12 passed a more advanced version (BC) that is usually administered after a student takes a second year of calculus. By 1990, Escalante's math enrichment program involved over 400 students in classes ranging from beginning algebra to advanced calculus.

Even more than his talent as a mathematician, Escalante's greatest trait is his ability to relate to all types of students and motivate them by raising their self-expectations. Incredibly, these teens forego Saturdays, evenings, and even summer holidays so they can develop their math skills and prepare to take the AP calculus exam.

One of the most important success beliefs is *ganas*. You must have a burning desire to succeed, or a "fire in your belly." If you lack the will to succeed, you'll probably be in the same rut years from now, looking for another book and wondering why it's always someone else who finds the success that you can't.

Goals Are Dreams with a Deadline

Mark Twain said, "Twenty years from now, you will be more disappointed by things you didn't try than by the ones you did. So throw off the bowlines. Sail away from the safe harbor. Catch the trade winds in your sails. Explore. Dream. Discover."[2]

There's Nothing Wrong with Very Ambitious Goals

David Clark caught the trade winds in his sails and demonstrated more perseverance than most of us will ever muster. On December 5, 1999, Clark set sail from Fort Lauderdale, Florida, in an attempt to circle the globe. The grandfather of six left Fort Lauderdale in a 42-foot sailboat in what was his third attempt to circle the planet. The journey was one that even the most experienced sailors would not undertake, let alone an elderly man.

The trip was not an easy one. Clark's beloved dog, Mickey, was lost at sea off the coast of South Africa. He encountered 25- to 30-foot waves, and sometimes, he would go a month without touching land. At one point, his boat sank and needed thousands of dollars in repairs. Remarkably, Clark became the oldest man to circle the globe under sail, returning home to Florida two years and two days after his departure.[3]

Whether you're crossing Antarctica by dogsled, crossing the globe by sailboat, or crossing the t's and dotting the i's on a new business plan, you can reach your goal through perseverance. There's an old Japanese proverb that says, "Get knocked down seven times, get up eight." And as long as you get up that eighth time, you'll eventually reach your goal. Vince Lombardi, the legendary Green Bay Packer coach, said, "The difference between a successful person and others is not a lack of strength, not a lack of knowledge, but rather a lack of will."[4]

Your goals should be realistic but not so easy that reaching them is a foregone conclusion. Your goals should force you to reach for something you might not generally be able to achieve.

A Message from Garcia

It is important to set goals. Don't set your goals so low that they are too easy to reach. Set your goals high enough so that they require you to work and to stretch yourself. This is how you improve and get better at doing certain things. Coasting down the hill is fun, but riding up along the ridge gives you the best view of all, and to reach it requires work. Regardless of your goals, the one ingredient that will give you the drive to achieve them is *ganas*. Nothing is impossible if you're burning with *ganas*, the fire in the belly, the passion you will need to remain steadfast in the pursuit of your dreams. *Ganas* will keep you focused when the going gets tough. This passion will help you attract the right people to help achieve your dreams and will help you overcome the most challenging obstacles.

CHAPTER 7

Success Belief 3:
Leave the Ivory Tower

SUCCESSFUL PEOPLE WEREN'T BORN WITH THE KNOWLEDGE THEY needed to achieve success. They acquired it. To acquire the knowledge and experience you need to succeed, you can't plant yourself in an ivory tower and remain isolated.

During my year as a White House Fellow, I worked at the Department of State for John Whitehead who was serving as the Deputy Secretary of State. Whitehead taught me that you couldn't do your job while sitting in your office. He urged me to learn how things get done in Washington. Whitehead, who began his career in the mailroom of Goldman Sachs after getting out of the Navy, was involved at the very highest levels of politics and business. Under his mentorship I learned to focus on the *process of government* instead of being blinded by the narrow issues that change as often as the weather. Issues change, the processes don't. He helped me understand the interrelationships between the Congress, the Executive Branch, the Judiciary, the press, the special interest groups, and the think tanks. I had to learn about the Washington bureaucracy from top to bottom. Each branch of the government had competing interests, from the career civil servants to the political appointees. I had to walk the halls of Congress, talking with career civil servants and political appointees at all levels of government. There's nothing like real-life experience to give you a true understanding and knowledge of how our government really works.

Outside the Ivory Tower, You Hear Different Perspectives

From the hallowed halls of Congress to the distant farmlands of Bolivian coca farmers, I always found that I learned a great deal from getting into the field. I spent part of my year at the U.S. State Department working in the Bureau of International Narcotics Matters, where I held a line job as the desk officer for Bolivia. I was stationed for a few weeks in Bolivia, and took part in field-work with Drug Enforcement Agency (DEA) agents and U.S. Army Special Forces green berets who were training their Bolivian counterparts to destroy drug labs and making helicopter runs on coca farmers.

The coca leaves used in making cocaine are often dried on huge cement circles that are about 50 yards wide. After drying on one side, the leaves are flipped over to further dry. Once fully dried, they are put in 100-pound sacks and transferred to the cocaine producers. To harass the farmers drying their coca leaves, the key to the production of cocaine, our Bolivian Air Force helicopter pilots would circle close to the ground, so the wind from the blades would scatter the drying coca leaves.

One hot summer afternoon, a pilot chose to land smack dab in the middle of one of those concrete circles and blasted the leaves everywhere. After we landed, I got out and approached the farmer who was drying these leaves. He was dressed in shorts with no shirt and was dirty from his hard work. His wife stood near him, a baby sucking on her breast and a young child tugging at her torn and ragged dress.

"Do you know that these leaves you're drying are used to make cocaine, which kills thousands of people in my country?" I said to him in Spanish.

"What country is that?" he asked, looking at me with his dark brown empty eyes, the eyes of a man beaten and defeated from hard work with little reward.

"The United States," I said. "We have crack babies dying, born to mothers addicted to cocaine." I continued with my lecture, adding details about the evils of drug trafficking, which undoubtedly meant nothing to him.

After I finished my speech, he stared at me for a moment. His wife was looking at me while gently rocking the child she held, the daughter clutching to her thigh and peering out from the side of her mother's dress, her big dark eyes not defeated, at least not yet like her father's or mother's.

"How many people in the United States die from cocaine?" asked the farmer.

I thought for a moment. "About 10,000 a year."

The farmer then pulled out a pack of Marlboros and asked me if I had a light. I didn't. He shrugged his shoulders, and emitted a smoker's cough, deep and retching. He managed to clear his throat and catch his breath. His wife and two children watched him perform this exercise, which they had probably heard a thousand times before. He finally spit out his words. "When I was a boy I wanted to grow up and be like the Marlboro man, I would see him on television," he said. "In fact I've been hooked on cigarettes for 20 years. I can't quit, even though I know it's going to kill me someday."

He then looked me straight in the eye and asked, "How many people in your country die from lung cancer from smoking cigarettes?"

"Probably around 200,000 or more," I said.

The farmer then pointed at the label on the pack. "Made in America," he said as though he was making some huge point, which I didn't get. "Mr. Gringo, when was the last time you landed a helicopter in a farmer's field in North Carolina?"

"I've never landed a helicopter in a farm field in North Carolina," I replied. "How many of these cigarettes does your country export to our country and all over the world?" he asked.

I thought for a moment. "I don't know," I said, "but probably a lot."

"Mr. Gringo, I'm just a farmer. I make $50 for a 100-pound bale of coca leaves, and I work a whole week for it so I can feed my family."

The farmer's response was jarring. For an uneducated man, he made a very powerful point. In his mind, he was doing nothing wrong. He was just a hard-working farmer trying to earn enough money to feed his family. He was simply growing an agricultural crop and selling it. Likewise, in the United States, from his point of view thousands of farmers grow millions of tons of tobacco plants and sell them to the tobacco manufacturers to make cigarettes, cigarettes that cause tremendous harm to untold millions of people.

From the Bolivian Coca Field to the Drug Czar's Office

My fieldwork in Bolivia came in handy when I was selected to work with former Secretary of Education William J. Bennett, who had just been appointed by President George H. W. Bush, to be the country's first Director of National Drug Control Policy, better known as the "Drug Czar." It was 1989 and I worked with Bennett and his staff to help draft the nation's first National Drug Control Policy, which became the blueprint for fighting the war against drugs in the United States. The policy was a broad-based strategy focused on four critical areas: treatment, education, prevention, and interdiction.

Bill Bennett is a perfect example of someone who knew the value of getting out from behind the desk, getting his hands dirty, and getting into the field. When he was Secretary of Education he visited more than 100 schools, asking tough questions and answering equally challenging ones from teachers and students.[1] By spending time in the classroom, Bennett was able to talk directly with teachers, rather than relying on union leaders for information.

On-the-Job Training Trumps the Theoretical Approach

We can learn from every person we meet and every experience we have. Education is obviously important, but skills also are acquired on the job. Jaime Escalante did not learn how to motivate disadvantaged students in education courses.[2]

Many law school graduates want to be corporate lawyers, yet they've had no experience handling complex transactions. These new attorneys know the legal principles governing complex corporate agreements, but have never drafted one. They're taught how to think like an attorney by professors who have never practiced law.

In my second year of law school, I was chosen for the Moot Court Editorial Board and became the mentor for 12 first-year law students. Instead of using a hypothetical case to help them develop their skills, I wanted my students to gain practical experience and work with a real legal situation. I learned of a case called *State v. Bamber*, which involved a significant search and seizure issue that was scheduled to be heard by the Florida Supreme Court.

With my students' help, I volunteered to work on the defendant's brief. I didn't stop there. I called Chief Justice Rosemary Barkette of the Florida Supreme Court and asked her if I could obtain the videotape of the oral arguments for this case. At that time, this practice was forbidden since the videotapes were for internal use only, so my initial requests were turned down. Eventually, she agreed to lend me the tape of the oral arguments, but only my students were allowed to view them.

The attorney handling the case also discussed it with my class. They were able to give him their thoughts on what arguments worked and didn't work, as well as offer suggestions on what other arguments he might have used in court. Afterward, I utilized all of that information and worked several more months on a law review article dealing with this topic.[3] The Florida Supreme Court ruled unanimously for the defendant and quoted from my law review article in their decision.

A Message from Garcia
....

Successful people leave the ivory tower and go out into the field. They get their hands dirty. They get out from behind their desks and see firsthand what it is that other people do in their organization. This helps them to gain a firsthand perspective of how things are done, opens the possibility of exploring new and better ways of doing things, and creates a valuable, credible and bonding experience with top executives, management and workers. It's easy to criticize others when you're watching from afar, but insightful to put yourself in someone else's place to see things from their perspective.

By seeing issues from different viewpoints, you'll be in a better position to make smart decisions. Each person you meet has the potential to provide insights that help you solve problems in your business and personal life. You might even latch onto a new idea for business or find the answer to a situation that's been bugging you for years. The person you least expect to be able to help might have something to say that changes your life.

CHAPTER 8

....

Success Belief 4:
Treat Everyone
You Meet as if
They Were a War Hero

WHEN YOU BELIEVE THAT EVERYONE HAS SOMETHING TO TEACH you, you're much more likely to treat everyone you meet with respect. Everyone has something to teach you if you're willing to listen. "Everyone" does in fact mean everyone; it doesn't matter what job someone has or if he or she speaks English with an accent. Henry David Thoreau said, "Heroes are often the most ordinary of men."

In my office, there's a large oil painting of William Crawford, a man I knew when I was a cadet at the Air Force Academy. He taught the cadets at the Air Force Academy a great deal, not just about respect, but also about leadership. Mr. Crawford was a squadron janitor. That's right. He was a janitor. For many years, he was a man who was taken for granted.

He mopped the floors and scrubbed the toilets. In the eyes of the cadets, what could be learned from him? To some of the cadets he was a nonentity, and to others he was an object of ridicule. All that changed one fall afternoon. James Moschgat, a cadet in the Class of 1977, was reading an incredible story about the tough Allied ground campaign in Italy during World War II. The book mentioned someone identified as Army private William Crawford, who was awarded the Congressional Medal of Honor for "conspicuous gallantry at risk of life above and beyond the call of duty."

The events took place four days after the invasion at Salerno in September 1943, during some of the bloodiest fighting in Italy. Private Crawford, a low-ranking Army squad scout assigned to the 36th Infantry Division, on three separate occasions saved his platoon when it was pinned down by intense enemy machine gun fire. Not only did he race through intense enemy fire to detonate hand grenades on enemy machine gun nests, but he also wrestled one of the enemy machine guns away and used it to fire on the withdrawing German commandos. Cadet Moschgat wondered if his janitor with the same name could be the very man who was thought killed for his heroic actions in Italy, and who posthumously received the Congressional Medal of Honor in 1944.

Although Mr. Crawford's father received his dead son's Congressional Medal of Honor in 1944, Private Crawford did not die that day. In fact, German soldiers captured him, and he was forced to march 500 miles in 52 days in the dead of winter to stay ahead of the advancing Russian army. He ended up in a German prisoner of war camp for two years until the end of the war. When the cadet confronted the janitor about this story, Mr. Crawford confirmed that he was in fact the man written about in the book. He was a Congressional Medal of Honor winner! Mr. Crawford told the cadet that after he retired as a master sergeant from the Army in 1967, he took the janitor's spot so he could teach future Air Force officers what he had learned from his experiences in the military.

In May 1984, President Ronald Reagan gave the commencement address at the U.S. Air Force Academy. At the conclusion of his remarks, President Reagan presented the Congressional Medal of Honor to William Crawford—this time personally as Presidents customarily do. Crawford passed away in 2000, and is the only

U.S. Army veteran and sole Medal of Honor winner to be buried in the cemetery of the Air Force Academy.

Mr. Crawford deserved respect because he was a part of the team and did a job that was no less important than anyone else's. Mr. Crawford had many valuable lessons to teach anyone who took the time to care. I keep a large painting of Mr. Crawford in my office to remind me that within everyone is the potential to be a hero. Not every person you meet will be a war hero. But if you want to be successful, treat everyone you meet with respect.

The POW Meets the Man
Who Packed His Parachute

Charles Plumb tells the story of being in a restaurant with his wife Cathy when he noticed a man at another table staring at him.[1] The man didn't look familiar, so Plumb ignored him. After a few more minutes, the man came over to their table and pointed his finger at Plumb. "You're Plumb," the stranger said.

"Yes, sir. I'm Plumb," he replied, despite having no idea who this man was.

"You flew fighter jets in Vietnam," the unidentified acquaintance declared. "You were on the aircraft carrier Kitty Hawk. You were shot down. You parachuted into enemy hands and spent six years as a prisoner of war."

Plumb was shocked. All this was true. Who could this gentleman be? After graduating from the Naval Academy in Annapolis, Plumb flew F-4 Phantom jets in Vietnam. After 74 successful combat missions, Plumb was shot down on his 75th, only five days before he was scheduled to return home. He was held in Communist prison camps for 2,103 days in an eight-by-eight foot cell.

Plumb finally found his voice. "How in the world did you know that?" he asked.

"I packed your parachute," the man replied as he shook Plumb's hand vigorously. "I guess it worked."

"It sure did," Plumb said. "If your chute hadn't worked, I wouldn't be here today." The chute was packed perfectly and saved Plumb's life. A surface-to-air missile hit Plumb's plane that day, forcing him and his copilot to eject at 500 miles per hour. They came floating down to earth in their perfectly packed parachutes. Unfortunately, the pilots landed in enemy territory and were captured as soon as they hit the ground.

When he returned home from the restaurant, Plumb kept visualizing the man and wondering what he might have looked like in his Navy uniform, with a white hat and bellbottom pants. He thought about how many times their paths crossed on the ship. Plumb wondered if he had snubbed the man because he was a hotshot fighter pilot and the man was just a sailor. The man's efforts saved Plumb's life, but Plumb may not have even acknowledged him.

Every day, dozens of people cross our paths and we may not be acknowledging their presence in any way. They may not be packing our parachutes, but they could be packing the wheel bearings in our car, packaging our food, or selling us a pack of gum. Regardless of their role in our lives, they are owed respect.

There's a Story Behind Every Person We Meet

Perhaps that homeless person we avoid eye contact with is a Vietnam vet, or someone suffering from mental illness or another ailment. The clerk with a thick foreign accent at the convenience store might have been a doctor, lawyer, or engineer before coming to this country.

If you keep an open mind, you'll find that everyone has something to teach you about business and life. Of course, it doesn't mean that you have to listen to every telephone solicitor who calls at dinnertime, but you should keep an open mind to different views and perspectives from the people you encounter.

Successful people feel that everyone, regardless of their position on the totem pole, has something to teach them. Throughout my career, I've given advice to generals and high-ranking people in government. Most of them listened to my analysis of a particular issue and felt I had something to offer. And I learned a great deal from junior officers, as well as enlisted men and women.

There will always be people who feel they don't have anything to learn. Try not to be one of them.

A Message from Garcia

Treat everyone you meet with respect; you have no idea who he or she may be, where they've been, and what they could contribute to your life. Maybe the person is a war hero, or a highly successful individual from another country who is here for any one of a number of reasons. There are lessons to be learned from everyone, whether it is humility, humor, or a gem of wisdom from someone who had it all and no longer does. You never know where the next idea or thought may come from that can change your life.

Think about how you treat others. Do you say hello or ignore them? Too often, we lose sight of the lessons we can learn from people around us. We tend to judge people too quickly based upon impression and, more often then not, insufficient evidence. Even though someone may not look like you, speak the same language as you, or have much money, they might have a wealth of experience from which you can learn.

Success Belief 5: Things Can Go from Bad to Great in the Blink of an Eye

THE SPIRITUAL LEADER REBBE NACHMAN SAID, "REMEMBER: THINGS can go from the very worst to the very best in the blink of an eye."[1] I believe you'll find that spirit of optimism in every successful person. Even when things are going bad, he or she knows things can get better at any moment.

One of my favorite stories involves two 8-year-old boys—one is an eternal optimist, and the other is an eternal pessimist. The boys are scheduled for an appointment with a noted psychologist. The psychologist specializes in treating children of this sort, those who are overly optimistic or pessimistic. As part of the treatment, the psychologist uses two rooms. One room is filled with video games and toys. The other room is filled knee-high with horse manure.

The psychologist puts the pessimist, Johnny, in the room with all the toys. He puts the optimist in the room with the horse manure. Two hours later, the psychologist comes in the room with all the toys and asks Johnny if he had fun. "No," Johnny replies. "I didn't play with any of them."

"Really? How come, Johnny? You have so many toys here. Couldn't you find anything you'd like to play with?" said the psychologist. Without skipping a beat, shuffling his feet, Johnny said, "Well, if I played with them I knew they'd just break, so I didn't."

The psychologist leaves and goes to the room where he left the eternal optimist. Much to the psychologist's surprise, the boy is busy; he cupped his hands together creating a makeshift shovel, and is now busy shoveling the manure over his shoulders, apparently enjoying himself. After a minute, the psychologist says to the boy, "What are you doing?"

The boy stops shoveling, looks at the psychologist, and says, "I know that with all of this horse manure, there must be a pony around here somewhere."

Success Takes More Than Luck

We all know people who see the glass half empty and believe that soon they'll have nothing to drink at all. Successful people hope and believe their luck will turn around at any moment. They would also agree with the words of Samuel Goldwyn, who said, "The harder I work, the luckier I get."

Speaking of luck, Paul Newman discussed some great advice he got from George Roy Hill, the director of *Butch Cassidy and the Sundance Kid*. When Newman said his success was based on luck, Hill told Newman, "Garbage—luck is an art. Luck marches right past most people. Their brains are too cross-eyed to notice."[2] Because of this advice, Newman came to realize, "It is possible to mess with luck, slow it down, hassle it, and maybe even overtake it."[3]

Success is about more than luck and hard work. In every community, you'll see restaurants go in and out of business. Often, at one particular location, you can count the number of restaurants that failed. All the restaurant owners worked hard, but couldn't make it work. Does that mean they were all unlucky? No, it means that more than likely, they picked the wrong location or the wrong chef, or their food and service wasn't distinguishable from a thousand other restaurants.

Hard work isn't a substitute for a good idea. If people aren't busting down the doors of the restaurant you open, try a different approach. Successful people continually look for new ideas and concepts or a new approach to improving their business, service, or product. Alexander Graham Bell said that when one door closes, another opens. Bell warned, however, that we spend so much time looking regretfully at the closed door that we fail to see the open ones.[4]

Heather Wilson, a former Air Force officer and the first female veteran to serve in Congress, said, "You will be touched by tragedy and triumph. Doors will appear that you do not even know are there."[5] So never, ever give up!

You Can Be an Optimist and a Realist

Although optimism and hope are extremely important, you also must be a realist. James Stockdale made that point to Jim Collins, the author of *Good to Great*. Stockdale told Collins that the optimists were the ones who didn't survive the POW camp in which he was imprisoned for eight long years. The optimists told themselves they would be out by Christmas or some other holiday. When that holiday came and went, the optimists died of a broken heart. Stockdale told Collins that although you can never afford to lose faith, you can't ignore the reality of your current situation.[6]

President Ronald Reagan was one of the world's great optimists. According to Colin Powell, Reagan's optimism had a positive influence on his cabinet. Even George Schultz worked hard to change his dour image and adopt Reagan's spirit of optimism. Powell believes optimism is a "force multiplier." It infuses the people around you with the same attitude. Conversely, Powell feels cynicism and negativity are "force shrinkers," which tend to demoralize everyone around you.[7]

All of us will face times in our lives when the optimism is sucked right out of us. You may lose your job, or your business will suffer a setback. Perhaps you're going through a divorce or you've lost someone you love deeply. Successful people have a tendency to recover quickly from those bleak moments and charge forward.

Eighty-two-year-old Ted Byram of Vero Beach, Florida, is a man who did just that. Byram, a bowling enthusiast, had a stroke. Did that sideline the octogenarian bowler? No way. Just 17 days after suffering a partial stroke and being temporarily unable to speak or lift his right arm, Byram was back at the lanes. What's more, he bowled a perfect game. Not bad for an 82-year-old guy! His recovery was amazing and his 12-strike game spectacular, considering his best score while healthy was 280.[8]

Even when the future looks bleak, good fortune may be a phone call away or around the corner. If you're looking down, it may walk right by you. But if you're looking up, you'll be ready to embrace it.

A Message from Garcia

Too many people give up when a door is closed in their face. More often than not, people are reluctant to jiggle the door handle even one more time to see if they can open it. Successful people are optimistic. Successful people do not dwell on the past or on the negative. They are positive that things will get better, and they keep hope alive. Optimism is the nourishment that fertilizes idea seedlings, allowing you the right attitude and mindset to cultivate them and the personal motivation to see them through to fruition.

CHAPTER 10

Success Belief 6: Honor, Duty, Country

ON MAY 12, 1962, GENERAL MACARTHUR MADE HIS LAST PUBLIC appearance at West Point, where he spoke to the cadets of the U.S. Military Academy and began with these words in a memorable tribute to the ideals that inspired that great American soldier:

Duty, honor, country—those three hallowed words reverently dictate what you want to be, what you can be, what you will be. They are your rallying point to build courage when courage seems to fail, to regain faith when there seems to be little cause for faith, to create hope when hope becomes forlorn. Unhappily, I possess neither that eloquence of diction, that poetry of imagination, nor that brilliance of metaphor to tell you all that they mean.[1]

The general prophesized that one day, should Americans forget to live by the great moral code of which he spoke, "A million ghosts in olive drab, in brown khaki, in blue and gray, would rise from their white crosses, thundering those magic words: duty, honor, and country."

One of the first principles I learned at the Air Force Academy was "Integrity First," then duty, then country. When you attend the Air Force Academy, the Naval Academy, West Point, or any other military-type institution, the honor code becomes your way of life. General H. Norman Schwartzkopf said that the honor code was the most important lesson drilled into him during his time at West Point.

Mike Krzyzewski, the head coach of the Duke University basketball team, credits West Point for his foundation as a coach, a leader, and a person. In 21 years at Duke, Coach Krzyzewski, an 11-time National Coach of the Year, with three national championships under his belt, has built a dynasty that few programs in the history of the game can match. Coach "K", as he is known, said, "Before I entered the academy, I thought I knew everything. I lived in my own protected little world. My parents had instilled in me a respect for authority and the ability to learn. But West Point took me to another level. I feel that I was very lucky to go there and get a good dose of honesty, honor, and discipline."[2]

Develop a Personal Honor Code

"We will not lie, steal or cheat, nor tolerate among us anyone who does." The words of the Cadet Honor Code are mounted in the granite stone above the west portal of the terrazzo adjacent to the cadet chapel at the U.S. Air Force Academy. In fact, while serving a Deputy Cadet Wing Commander and Chairman of the Cadet Wing Honor Committee at the Air Force Academy in 1983, I played a key role in getting those words onto the granite wall so that every cadet would be subconsciously encouraged to internalize this minimum standard of personal integrity.

The decisions and choices you make in life might be much simpler if you adopt and abide by an honor code of your own. If you were a cadet today at the Air Force Academy, you would be taken to the Honor Court wall and made to swear allegiance to an "honor oath." The oath simply states, "We will not lie, steal or cheat, nor tolerate among us anyone who does. Furthermore, I resolve to do my duty and to live honorably, so help me God." This oath recognizes that honor has a broader meaning than simply not lying, stealing, or cheating. True honor requires righteous actions rather than simple abstinence from wrongdoing. We also believe that tolerating cheating, or some other violation of the Honor Code, is every bit as wrong as committing the infraction itself. The cadet who knows of a violation and does not report it has also broken the Honor Code and could be expelled. The Honor Code is a vital part of a cadet's character development and the foundation upon which each cadet builds a personal notion of professional ethics and a minimum standard of integrity. The Honor Code also gives privileges to each cadet. A cadet's word is accepted as the truth at all times. Adhering to the code fosters a feeling of mutual trust that grows throughout their time at the Academy and hopefully provides a dimension of ethical maturity that serves them throughout their lives.

Chairman of the Cadet Honor Committee is at once a revered and reviled position, which requires the fortitude to make very tough decisions about friends and peers. During my tenure as Honor Chairman I focused on three key areas, that I called the three E's: Education, Environment, and Enforcement.

Education
This was the most important focus of my efforts. I paid special attention to the educational classes cadets received on the importance of the Honor Code throughout their student careers at the Academy. These classes are the equivalent of an academic course and continue each semester throughout the four years; they cover the Honor Code as it applies to their life at the Academy, officership, the Air Force, and service to the country. The focus is on formal classroom presentations, guest speakers, and informal discussions directed at these habits of honorable behavior as the foundations of the military profession.

Environment
The code demands absolute integrity in one's words and one's actions. Cadets are expected to report themselves for any infraction of the Honor Code, and the nontoleration clause demands that they confront any cadet they believe may have violated the code and

report the incident if the situation is not resolved. Although not an easy standard, living in a community that accepts it creates an environment of trust unparalleled at other academic institutions. Because the leaders at the Air Force Academy believe that character can be taught and developed, we worked hard to create an environment of trust and respect. During my tenure we unlocked all the doors in the cadet dormitory. Why should we lock the doors when we had an Honor Code to protect us? We also convinced the leadership of the Air Force Academy that the Honor Code should be boldly displayed in the cadet area so everyone could see it, and plans were put in place to put it in an appropriate location on a wall.

Enforcement

Despite the Academy's emphasis on integrity, some cadets put themselves in situations where their honor is called into question. If a violation of the Honor Code is suspected, an investigative team is appointed to gather relevant evidence about the suspected honor violation. The investigation concludes with a review of all evidence to determine if the case should be forwarded to a Wing Honor Board. If a cadet self-reports a violation or admits one when confronted, the case is sent to a Cadet Sanctions Recommendation Panel.

The Wing Honor Board is conducted in an atmosphere similar to a legal proceeding, but the proceedings are not adversarial in nature. The suspected cadet is present during all testimony and may ask questions of any witness. There is no requirement for testimony by the suspected cadet, but most do decide to testify in their own behalf. According to the current procedures, a jury of seven cadets and one officer, all selected at random, hears and reviews all evidence and testimony under the guidance of the nonvoting Chairperson. Following the presentation of all evidence and closed deliberations, the Wing Honor Board votes by secret ballot for or against a violation. For a cadet to be found guilty, at least six of the eight voting members of the jury must be convinced beyond a reasonable doubt that their was an act that violated the Honor Code, and the cadet had the requisite intent.

The presumptive sanction for an Honor Code violation is expulsion. However, under certain circumstances this recommendation may be suspended and the cadet placed on honor probation. If the commandant's recommendation is for expulsion, the case will be sent to the superintendent. At any point during the honor process, the cadet may elect to resign.

The Honor Committee that I oversaw in 1982–83 conducted 250 investigations and convened 108 Honor Boards. I personally sat on 72 Honor Boards, which was like being a judge, overseeing the eight jurors selected at random from the cadet wing. Evidence was presented and witnesses were called. In my quasi-judicial role on the Honor Board, I participated in the questioning of witnesses. I also sat in and helped guide the jury deliberations. Unfortunately, 60 of those 108 cadets were expelled from the Academy.

One cadet, a friend of mine, graduated from school and was waiting to participate in graduation ceremonies. As his parents were driving across the country to the ceremonies, he received a visit from old high school friends. He took his friends on a tour of the Academy and showed them the cadet wing dormitory, even though no one except cadets and Air Force personnel is allowed in the cadet wing dormitory.

When the cadet brought his friends to the dormitory, an underclassman stopped them and challenged their right to enter. The graduating cadet pulled out his identification and lied, saying that the visitors were Air Force personnel. The underclassman allowed them access because of the graduating cadet's assurance that they were authorized visitors, yet he turned them in to an Honor Committee representative because he suspected the upperclassman of lying.

The graduating cadet committed an Honor Code violation by lying to the underclassman. An Honor Board was convened and the graduating cadet was expelled. The graduating cadet got his academic degree, but never became an officer. Nevertheless, he did serve his five-year commitment to the Air Force as an enlisted person.

Whether you agree with the punishment or not, we lived by the Honor Code and everyone knew how important it was to follow the code. During lunch meal formation, we would submit and read to the entire 4,000-cadet wing the Cadet X and Cadet Y letters, explaining why someone was expelled or disciplined. We would read them over the loud speaker prior to the noontime meal so that everyone understood the ramifications of violating the Honor Code.

The Supreme Quality of a Leader

Unfortunately, in today's business world honor is often just a buzzword and many leaders can't be taken at their word. It is impossible to lead if you have no credibility with the people you do business with, and your employees don't have faith in your integrity. If you don't think it's important for a business to act with integrity, take a look at Merrill Lynch. The company agreed to pay $100 million in penalties to settle charges that its analysts misled investors. Merrill Lynch analysts rated certain stocks as good buys in order to gain more business for the firm's investment bankers. Merrill Lynch investment bankers handled mergers and initial public stock offerings for these companies, which was a huge source of revenue for the firm.[3]

Recently, we've seen many companies destroyed because of a lack of integrity and honor. Among their other sins, the leaders at Enron betrayed their employees, their stockholders, and the public. Arthur Andersen's reputation was permanently smeared by its handling of Enron's financial matters. As a result, one of the world's largest companies and one of the world's premier accounting firms was ruined. WorldCom executives also mislead shareholders and employees. WorldCom falsified its profits by misreporting $3.8 billion in expenses. Fabrications by WorldCom and other companies caused a crisis of confidence and trust among investors.

These transgressions of integrity and honesty occurred not just in the private sector, but in government as well. FBI leaders lost the trust of many employees because of their failure to admit mistakes in investigating terrorism. Initially, the FBI downplayed its failure to follow significant leads that might have prevented the terrorist attacks on September 11, 2001. Many FBI leaders glossed over key facts to avoid personal and institutional embarrassment.

Integrity could have kept John J. Rigas, the founder of Adelphia Communications, and his family from being arrested. According to prosecutors, Rigas and his family used the company as if it was their personal piggybank. At one point, Rigas allegedly took over $66 million in advances from the company. Rigas and certain family members have been accused of many white-collar crimes.

President Dwight D. Eisenhower said, "The supreme quality for a leader is integrity."[4] Integrity and honor are qualities that are important to anyone who wants to be successful.

Ethics Are More Than Words in the Employee Handbook

Whether in the private sector, in the government, or in any hierachical organization, leaders must show those who look up to them that ethics are important. This is a prime case of "do as I do" and not just "as I say." Leaders must reinforce the company's ethical standards. It's not enough to put them in an employee handbook. Penalties for violating the rules must be enforced with more than a slap on the wrist.

Basketball coach Rick Pitino hit the nail on the head when he said, "You can make mistakes and be forgiven, but dishonesty lingers in people's minds forever. It is much easier to keep your reputation than it is to rebuild it. Lying makes a problem part of your future; truth makes a problem part of your past."[5]

No matter what position you occupy in your organization, you can act with a strong sense of integrity. The cashier who acts with integrity will correct the elderly customer who inadvertently overpays for an item and leaves without his or her change.

Have you ever played golf with a person who cheats? Or have you played tennis with someone who calls a ball out that you know is in? Under no circumstances would I want to do business with someone like that! If someone is lying or cheating during a game or a social sport, then how will he or she perform during the "war" that business can be?

There's a story about golfer Babe Zaharias that illustrates the type of person she was. She accidentally played the wrong ball in a major tournament and penalized herself two strokes, even though no one knew. Zaharias was asked later why she turned herself in, since no one was aware of her mistake. To the honorable and talented Zaharias, it was moot that no one else knew of her mistake. All that mattered was that she knew she inadvertently had violated the rules.[6]

Teach Your Children the Value of Integrity

Good parenting is essential if you want your children to grow up and be decent human beings. Teach your children about courtesy, empathy, and compassion. Teach your children these lessons, and you will have taught them well. Trust the teachers with algebra, history, and grammar. Well-mannered, well-behaved, considerate people will go far, even if they are average, or even below average, students. Why? Because people will like them, and people always prefer to do business with those they like, trust, or believe to be good human beings. What lessons are you teaching your children about integrity? Do they see you playing hooky from work? When they need school supplies, do you do your shopping at the office supply cabinet?

Before her death, the popular advice columnist Ann Landers reprinted letters about people who complained about shoppers in a grocery store who graze on produce while shopping. A grocery store manager reports that he finds empty soda cans on shelves, as well as cupcakes missing from packages.[7] In response to the letters, Ann Landers wondered if people view these thefts as no big deal. Children should be getting the message that every theft is a big deal, and that includes eating food and snacks off the shelves of grocery stores while walking through the isles. There are simply no excuses for that kind of behavior. These lessons on integrity are taught in the homes of successful people.

A Message from Garcia

Integrity. Honor. Trust. These are essential character traits if you want people to like you and if you want people to do business with you. If you are a CEO, your employees will demand this of you, and if you are building a company, your customers will seek these traits in you. By acting honorably and being forthright, consistent, and fair, customers and employees alike will respect your decisions.

All leaders must set the moral compass of their organization. Every employee should have a clear understanding of what conduct is acceptable, and what is not. Anyone who crosses that line should be disciplined. It is important that everyone in the company be aware that lapses in integrity or moral conduct will not be tolerated.

In your personal life you should also adhere to the character traits that your children will admire, learn from, and respect. By acting with honor and integrity, you build trust. Your actions must be consistent with your words. Saying the right thing doesn't mean anything unless you do the right thing. True honor requires righteous action rather than simple abstinence from wrongdoing. Each and every one of us can act and live by these concepts. If you see someone drop money or a personal object, for example, get their attention and give it back to them. Maybe you borrowed a book from someone and have had it for a long time. Whether you've read it or not, return it. They'll be grateful and think better of you, and might be likely to loan you another book.

Success Belief 7: Always Do What Is Right, and Let the Chips Fall Where They May

WHEN I HAVE TO ASSESS A BUSINESS OR OTHER ISSUE, I THOROUGHLY research the subject, analyze the data, and present my findings, regardless of the impact on a particular person, position, or situation. I took this approach in analyzing the culprits of the anthrax attacks after September 11, 2001, in analyzing the Chinese air defense system, in analyzing Cuba's support of insurgent movements in Latin America, and in analyzing the rise of drug traffickers and their link to guerrilla movements. I take this same approach in my company, Sterling Financial Investment Group, which has an exceptional reputation as a research firm that specializes in the health care and biotech sectors. We pride ourselves on publishing unbiased research. After doing research and investigating companies that we cover, we report the truth, regardless of the consequences.

I believe this is rare in the world of financial services and investment banking because many investment banking companies such as ours, who provide research coverage on other companies and report those results to the public, have a vested interest in the recommendations they publish. Consequently, a lopsided percentage of research reports are on the *buy* side, which is always favorable to the company. This either ensures that the company's stock remains in a *status quo* state, or better yet, rises because of the reports that these investment banking firms publish. When research is biased, you wind up with favorable evaluations of companies such as Enron, WorldCom, ImClone, and others. As we have seen, those stocks were hyped and overinflated. As a result, truth was camouflaged, along with the real facts about these companies' position in the market place. Ultimately, the consequences of this false reporting contributed directly to their own collapse and to the loss of billions of dollars for consumers, pension funds, and retirees. Literally millions of Americans' savings were wiped out and retirement funds depleted.

The alternative is for investment banking companies to publish *sell* recommendations. However, there is a natural reluctance on the part of investment banking companies to publish sell recommendations. As the American public discovered first hand, publishing anything other than a buy recommendation hurts a company's stock, and that in turn affects the investment bankers who cover the firm and whose salaries are often tied to the financial performance of the company itself—a conflict of interest if ever there was one. This, by the way, has been corrected. All relationships must now be fully disclosed, and who gets what is now a matter of public information. No doubt this will go a long way toward correcting some of these problems.

In Wall Street, sell recommendations constitute only 0.5 percent of all research recommendations. Our firm has been willing to put out sell recommendations, which doesn't make us very popular in some circles. Our track record over the last four years has been extraordinary, and we now count as clients nearly 300 of the largest and most active mutual fund and hedge fund managers in the country. Due to this large client list, when we initiate research coverage of a public company with a "Sell" it sometimes causes the company's stock to drop up to 15 percent the day we issue the report. Not only does the company have to immediately call an analyst conference that day to refute our analysis, but they then begin to threaten our company with lawsuits and spurious allegations of wrongdoing to the National Association of Securities Dealers (NASD), which regulates our industry. The NASD is often forced to investigate, and it becomes a costly battle that places our analysts under a microscope, one that analysts churning out "Buy" after "Strong Buy" report are rarely under themselves. In fact, during 2002, we issued sell recommendations on 50 percent of the companies we covered.

Long before Martha Stewart sold her shares of ImClone stock and was accused of insider trading, Sterling Financial reviewed all the published reports on Imclone, including those from their management team, and consulted with our own top cancer specialists in the field. We came away with a very different take on the future of the company. Our firm was the first major Wall Street investment bank to issue a sell recommendation on the company.

Don't Be Afraid to Give Bad News

As I mentioned earlier, I assisted Bill Bennett, the former Secretary of Education and Drug Czar, in drafting the nation's first National Drug Control Strategy. The strategy was a comprehensive blueprint to fight the spread of drugs in the United States. The report gave the cold, hard facts, and did not attempt to minimize the magnitude of the drug-trafficking problem, regardless of whose feathers might get ruffled in the process.

I enjoyed working for Bill Bennett because he was a roll-up-your-sleeves-and-pop-up-the-hood kind of guy. He wants to see how the engine works. According to Bennett, you need to learn as much as you can about a particular issue and go head-to-head with those who hold a different position. You can't be afraid to tell the truth, even if your position isn't very popular. Bennett believes that the American public is smart and will arrive at the right conclusion if given the facts. He also believes that Americans are capable of understanding the gravity of issues without panicking.

Regardless of the political implication, Bennett took action. The day after becoming the Drug Czar, he called for a ban on assault rifles, a major and very controversial act, which raised a furor. But Bennett knew how to get people's attention. Bennett also thought it was hypocritical to declare a war on drugs from Washington, D.C., a city that had drug dealers on every corner. He spearheaded a $150 million initiative to attack the drug problem in the nation's capitol.

Like all of us, Bennett is not perfect. While he has long admitted publicly to a taste for gambling, he's no hypocrite. When he became Drug Czar, Bennett gave up his 2½-pack-per-day smoking habit. When the media recently reported he enjoyed high stakes gambling, Bennett did not dodge the issue, he faced it head-on. Even though he is not a public official, and broke no laws, he admitted that gambling was wrong, that he had a problem, and he promised to stop. Certainly Bennett's effort to promote moral standards in public life and to teach our children the difference between right and wrong has not lost any of its validity.

A Message from Garcia

Tell the truth. Be vigilant and diligent when doing research, analysis and investigation or when compiling the facts on a problem or situation. In business and personal relationships, be honest with people, whether the news is good or bad. The final analysis may hurt but people will respect you for being honest, especially if your observations are meant genuinely and delivered without malice. Acting in this manner contributes greatly to your integrity, honor, and trust. When people understand how you approach a decision, they are more inclined to accept it, even if they don't like it. Apply this approach to all decision making, at work and at home. You will be amazed how quickly people around you will begin to value your judgment and seek your advice.

CHAPTER 12

Success Belief 8: Reading Is a Magnet for Success

WHEN I WAS GROWING UP IN PANAMA, MY FATHER USED TO READ history books to us. He was a doctor, but he knew more about American politics and government than most people born in the United States. His close friend, General Omar Torrijos, the Panamanian leader from 1968–1981, sought his counsel because of his tremendous political knowledge. In fact, my father was at the side of Torrijos when he negotiated with President Jimmy Carter for the return of the Panama Canal.

When I worked for General Galvin at the time he was the commander of the U.S. Southern Command, he read one or two books each week. The General preferred biographies of successful people or books that covered issues that he needed to understand. For example, if we were headed for Peru, he would read books by the top authors in Peru. By doing so, the General knew as much about the culture as possible before we began our operations. It also helped that Galvin could speak Spanish.

General Galvin also taught me how to read a book more effectively. He said you should not read a nonfiction book without having a pen in hand. At the end of the book, assuming it's yours, you should make notes about what you learned. By having a summary at the back of the book, you can easily refresh your recollection of what you learned. It also helps to put a page reference for each nugget of information, so you easily can refer back to the appropriate section of the book.

Reading Helps You Build Confidence and Self-Esteem

Reading—and the knowledge that comes from it—can help you gain confidence and build self-esteem. Reading has been at the core of any success that I have achieved. Take my work in the military, for example. When I was a 24-year-old second lieutenant, government officials and a four-star general listened to what I had to say. I was an analyst; my job was to read military reports and distill them down to present to the general's staff every single morning. To prepare the military analysis, I didn't just look at military reports as most analysts did. I read every scrap of paper I could find and I also called journalists to get their read on what was going on. My audience listened because I had read more on this particular military matter than nearly anyone else, and they knew I would do a thorough analysis based on the available information. Reading gave my advice credibility.

In 1983, I prepared a detailed analysis of China's air defense capabilities and recommended countermeasures. In 1984, I conducted an analysis of the Third World debt crisis. In 1985 and 1986, I analyzed guerrilla warfare and terrorism in Latin America. As a White House Fellow, I analyzed U.S. narcotics countermeasures. During the preparation of those analyses, I read every scrap of paper I could find on those subjects. Today, when my company analyzes an investment, we read every document we can find about a company and every bit of information we can glean from the Internet.

Another military commander, who was a U.S. president, also believed in the importance of reading and knowledge. Abraham

Lincoln used every opportunity he had to read. Despite his lack of a formal education, Lincoln developed much of his self-esteem from reading. It gave him confidence to face Stephen Douglas in their great debate and the knowledge Lincoln needed to interact with the generals he commanded during the Civil War.[1] According to historian William Lee Miller, Abraham Lincoln made a lifelong habit of cultivating his mind. Lincoln grew up in Little Pigeon Creek, a rural community in Indiana where few people learned to read. Yet Lincoln was often seen with a book in his hands as he walked down the dirt road.[2]

Lincoln would read during breaks from all of his jobs, whether he was splitting rails, watching the store, working as a postmaster, or farming. When he was President, Lincoln read military histories so he could stay on an equal plane with his generals. For a long time, Lincoln deferred to people with more formal education. He compared his mind to a piece of steel. Lincoln said his mind "was very hard to scratch anything on it, and almost impossible after you get it there to rub it out."[3]

Lifelong Learning Can Help Your Business

Whatever your business, you can learn from everyone on the totem pole. Sam Walton, founder of Wal-Mart, said, "Our best ideas have come from clerks and stock boys."[4] Listening to their advice helped Walton become one of the richest men in America, and Walton helped many of his employees become wealthy through innovative profit-sharing plans.

John P. Kotter, author of *Leading Change* and a professor at the Harvard Business School, says that the key to creating and sustaining the twenty-first-century organization is leadership at the top of the hierarchy, as well as leadership throughout the enterprise.[5] The leaders of the twenty-first-century organization will develop their skills through lifelong learning. Kotter says these leaders don't necessarily begin the race with the most money or intelligence, but outgrow their rivals. They learn to be leaders.[6]

Herb Kelleher, former president of Southwest Airlines, was a strong proponent of lifelong learning. Each major work area at Southwest has its own training department. At Southwest's "people department," numerous courses are offered to help employees develop their skills. The program is called "University for People."[7]

John P. Kotter says that people who strive to learn throughout their lifetime have high standards, ambitious goals, and a genuine sense of mission in their lives. Their goals and aspirations spur them on. They view their accomplishments from a humble perspective. Sometimes, their mission is developed when they're young. Sometimes, it happens during adulthood. Their aspirations keep them from becoming complacent.[8]

I'm Too Busy Is No Excuse for Not Learning

Lifelong learning means being better informed about what's going on in the world and making better use of the time you do have. You can listen to a book-on-tape while you're commuting to work. Put on FOX News, CNN, MSNBC, the Discovery Channel, or public television for a few minutes, instead of watching that "Seinfeld" rerun for the seventh time or flicking from station to station with the remote control. Learn a new language with language tapes while you're working out at the gym.

At work, instead of standing around the water cooler gossiping or complaining, use that time to learn something new, interesting, and valuable. Talk to a coworker who's from another country and learn something interesting about his or her culture. You can even try to learn a few phrases from that person's native language. These discussions may contribute to your knowledge of geography. It surprises me how little most people know about where certain countries are located. I live in Florida and am frequently amazed at how many local people don't know if Haiti is in the Caribbean or near the Philippines.

As you get older, you can continue to learn. Retirement experts have observed that many retirees choose to settle in college towns.

One reason for this is that they are able to take courses at local colleges and universities. Their thirst for knowledge stays with them as they age, and this helps them remain vibrant. A study for *My Generation*, an AARP publication, found that 6 of 10 baby boomers are always trying to learn new things.[9]

A Message from Garcia

All great leaders are readers—they have a love of learning and a deep well of intellectual curiosity they constantly yearn to fill. Reading can give anyone an enormous edge in any endeavor. Regardless of who you are and what you do, reading can help you gain confidence and build self-esteem; it will provide you with the ability to talk with anyone in any situation, whether you read the newspaper every day, or books. You can find ways to expand your knowledge by using your time more creatively. For example, listen to a book on tape while in the car instead of the radio. People who love to learn are open to new ideas. They rarely reject the notion of change because they have "always done something a certain way." Ben Franklin's intellectual curiosity helped him become an inventor, publisher, and statesman. Franklin said, "An investment in knowledge pays the best interest."[10] Without a doubt, the most successful people I know possess a genuine intellectual curiosity. They have what Jaime Escalante calls a *ganas* for learning.

······································

CHAPTER 13

Success Belief 9:
You Don't Fail
If You Learn a Lesson
and Persevere

FOR A LONG TIME, DESPITE BEING A MULTIMILLIONAIRE, STEVE Fossett was viewed as a failure. Over the course of several years, Fossett attempted to become the first person to fly around the world solo in a hot-air balloon. The 58-year-old multimillionaire failed five times and almost lost his life while trying. During his first flight in 1998, his balloon was ruptured in a thunderstorm that caused him to plunge into the Coral Sea, 500 miles off the coast of Australia.

On his sixth attempt, however, Fossett became the first balloonist to circle the world by himself. He navigated the balloon for 13½ days and over 19,000 miles. Fossett survived violent thunderstorms and outside temperatures of -50°F. He slept in a room the size of a prison cell, lived off some survivor food called MREs, and used a bucket for a toilet.

Fossett was able to achieve his goals because he learned from his previous failures. Each unsuccessful attempt taught him something new about what he needed to do differently. He improved the design of the balloon and benefited from improvements in weather forecasting. Fossett isn't resting on his laurels, either. His next endeavor is to fly a glider into the stratosphere. The glider will take him 60,000 feet above southern New Zealand.[1]

John C. Maxwell, author of *Failing Forward: Turning Mistakes Into Stepping Stones*, says, "The difference between average people and achieving people is their perception of and response to failure."[2]

Failure Is in the Eyes of the Beholder

As Maxwell suggested in *Failing Forward*, failure is in the eyes of the beholder. Let's say Steven Spielberg's latest movie tanks and barely recovers its investment. Does that make Spielberg a failure? Hardly.

Everyone's perception of success and failure is different. One director may view his movie as a failure because it only pulled in $100 million in box office receipts. Another director, whose films barely break even, would love to make a movie that "failed" like that. How about an actor who only gets roles in commercials? Is he a failure, because he never gets a role in a movie? To many aspiring actors and actresses, he's a recognizable face on television, he's working and making money, and he's indeed very successful. Who decides if a book is a success or a failure, the critics or the public? And even if the book doesn't sell very well, think of the many aspiring authors who would be thrilled just to see their manuscript in print.

Now let's take a look at an executive who works at a major corporation. She is so very close to the top, but never makes CEO, a position she's wanted since joining the company 20 years ago. Does that make her a failure? All of these issues go into your perception of failure and how you respond to it. Maxwell distinguishes between failing backward and failing forward. Failing backward is negative. Failing forward is how achievers make progress toward their goals. Legendary baseball slugger Babe Ruth said, "Never let the fear of striking out get in your way."

Successful People Don't Make the Same Mistake Twice

Whether it's marriage, business, or life in general, successful people don't repeat their mistakes. They learn from those mistakes and make better decisions based on what they've learned.

I've seen businesses that rehire a mediocre employee because they're desperate for a body to fill a position or they don't want to train someone new. These businesses settle for less than the best person because they lack the energy or the confidence to seek out someone better.

In his book *Success Is a Journey*, Jeffrey J. Mayer points out that successful people have the courage to admit they've made a mistake. They don't waste time, energy, and resources defending a mistake or bad decision.[3] Admiral Stockdale is a believer that successful people don't make the same mistake twice because they're always improving themselves. They move forward, armed with the knowledge they've gained from continual self-improvement.

John Maxwell said, "If at first you do succeed, try something harder."[4]

A Message from Garcia
··

Whether you're trying to fly your country's flag at the top of a mountain, fly around the world in a balloon or plane, or pilot your company to the number one spot on any business list, you will not be able to achieve exceptional success if you are afraid of failure. Never fear failure. In fact, failure doesn't even belong in your vocabulary, and you should equate it with a mistake, a temporary setback on your way to success. As long as you learn from your mistake, you can chalk it up to a valuable learning experience. People stumble all the time on their way to success, but only those who can get up, dust themselves off, and persevere eventually succeed.

Successful people make mistakes all the time. It comes with the territory of trying to achieve exceptional goals, or a sensational achievement. The difference is that successful people become successful by learning from their mistakes. They look at a failure as an opportunity to learn from what went wrong and how they can do something better, or different, to continue on the path to the achievement of that goal or dream.

The key to controlling failure is trying not to make the same mistake twice. Too many people beat themselves up for making a mistake and become less decisive, or worse, disheartened, and choose not to pursue their goals. What counts is where you are now and what you have gained from the experience. Successful people continue to focus on reaching their destination, even if they're a little behind schedule.

CHAPTER 14

Success Belief 10: Serve Your Community and Reap the Rewards

IN 2001, WHEN GOVERNOR JEB BUSH ASKED ME TO SERVE ON THE newly created Florida Board of Education, which is responsible for setting policy in Florida for all public education and interfacing with private education, I knew it would take an enormous amount of time. However, the stakes were too high for me to say no. I had been given a tremendous opportunity to make a real difference in the lives of Florida children and students.

My desire to give back to the community stems from my upbringing. My grandfather, Dr. A. M. McCarthy, was a former Daytona Beach city commissioner and Volusia County commissioner who helped to build the first integrated hospital in Daytona Beach. He frequently told me, "Always give back. Don't ask for anything. Just do it. It comes back to you tenfold."

General Torrijos always asked his wife what my father, Dr. Carlos Garcia, wanted from public service. What he enjoyed most was the honor and privilege of being able to whisper advice in the general's ear. By helping to shape the country's future he was rewarded in ways that are far more important than money.

As a result of this upbringing, I now strongly believe in contributing to the community, no matter where I may be living. In 1984 and 1985, I was on a temporary duty assignment in Honduras for the Strategic Air Command. My principle responsibility as Senior Intelligence Watch Officer was to analyze current activities in Nicaragua, Honduras, and El Salvador. Since I worked the late night shift and was off during the day, I volunteered and became a permanent member of the Medical Readiness Team (MEDRETE). The MEDRETE traveled throughout Honduras to provide medical services to remote communities. Three times each week, doctors, nurses, veterinarians, medics, dentists, and interpreters left Palmerola Air Base in Central Honduras aboard UH-60 Black hawks and CH-47 Chinooks.

Each trip to an isolated Honduran village was an adventure. A military policeman with an M-60 machine gun watched for trouble as the convoy of helicopters moved into increasingly remote territory. After a flight that would last anywhere from one to two hours, we would arrive at our destination, such as the tiny mountain village of El Triunfo, too small to be on any map and near the Nicaraguan border. Wherever we arrived in this massive army helicopter, a large crowd would always greet us. People from miles away came to see the *medicos*.

By 9:00 in the morning, the heat would be unbearable. It also didn't help that hundreds of horses, mules, burros, pigs, and dogs came to our mobile clinic. The human misery was difficult to watch. Many Honduran children suffered from malnutrition, and most of them had worms and parasites from drinking filthy water and bathing in streams that were little more than open sewers. Birth defects went uncared for. I remember a little boy with one arm, bowed legs, and feet turned under. Unable to stand, he scooted along the ground on his one hand, dragging his feet behind. Adults were not in much better shape. Broken bones had gone unset, minor cuts often became infected, and malaria was widespread.

Because I was fluent in Spanish, my job was to act as the pharmacist. On every mission, I passed out over 400 prescriptions. Making sure those prescriptions were administered properly was not easy. Imagine an illiterate mother of five who needs different medicines for each child, and neither she nor anyone else in her community can read the prescription. Since 90 percent of the patients were illiterate, I created picture cards to explain the required dosage. These medical trips were especially significant for me because the medical care often made the difference between life and death. For the people we helped, our military uniforms symbolized life and good will.

From Honduras to Palm Beach County

Today, the bulk of my public service is in the area of education. I first got involved in my local immunity when the Superintendent of the Palm Beach County School System forced an award-winning principal and educator, Dr. Art Johnson, to quit his administrative post in 1997. The timing couldn't have been worse. I had just started my company and really couldn't afford any distractions. Nevertheless, after hearing the facts surrounding Dr. Johnson's dismissal, I couldn't sit still. I helped launch an aggressive campaign to have him reinstated. I felt Johnson was the victim of a grave injustice, and as a result the quality of education in Palm Beach County would greatly suffer.

Along with legal maneuvering on Johnson's behalf, I later decided to help manage what would become a successful campaign for his appointment to the school board. I spent countless hours working on his behalf, time that might have been better spent working on my own business. Ultimately, several years later, Johnson successfully voted to dismiss the superintendent that fired him and shortly thereafter he became the superintendent of the Palm Beach County school system.

When I made the decision to help Johnson, I knew it would take time away from my business at a rather crucial time. Eventually, I benefited professionally and personally from waging the battle on Johnson's behalf. My *pro bono* efforts helped me build relationships with important members of the community, and I have gained the friendship and trust of many good people. I also know that our educational system is improving because Johnson, the finest educator I know, is now in charge.

Remember, giving to the community always has a way of coming back to you. You might meet another volunteer and develop a lifetime friendship or a fantastic business relationship. Ultimately, you make the community a better place for yourself and your children.

The Hispanic Community

I have focused much of my community involvement on helping Hispanic Americans. Data from the 2000 Census shows that Hispanics are the fastest-growing minority group. In 2020, one of every five American residents will be Hispanic. By the year 2050, one in every four Americans will be of Hispanic descent. The Hispanic community grew by nearly 60 percent in the past decade. These figures are too large for any leader or company to ignore.

In 2002, Hispanics represented the single largest minority group in the country with a population of nearly 43.8 million. Unfortunately, while Hispanic Americans have made huge strides, they are not yet empowered. They are not empowered because Hispanics lack adequate representation in federal and state governments, in the U.S. Congress, and also in the private sector, specifically as board members of this nation's largest corporations. For example, Hispanics hold only 1.4 percent of Fortune 1000 board seats. Yet they account for nearly 10 percent of the private sector workforce.

This is why improving education for Hispanics is crucial. Sadly, Hispanic children have an extremely low graduation rate, with over 30 percent dropping out of a high school. As the only Hispanic member of Florida's State Board of Education, I have made it one of my goals to improve these disheartening statistics, not just for Hispanics, but also for all minorities. Likewise, on a national level, my work for President George W. Bush on the Commission for Educational Excellence for Hispanic Americans provides me an opportunity to make a direct impact on national policy to improve educational opportunities for Hispanic American children in schools throughout the country.

Stop Making Excuses

According to a study in the AARP publication *My Generation*, 83 percent of baby boomers say they wish they could do good deeds for other people. Well, now is the time to stop talking and act upon your desire to help[1].

The same study found that 6 of 10 boomers wish their life had more meaning. When you finally get around to doing that good deed, you'll find a lot more meaning in your life. Instead of putting it off or talking in the abstract about helping others, get involved with one charity or cause that you believe in strongly. Help could even be needed right in your neighborhood.

Actor Paul Newman has been giving back to the community for over 20 years. In 1982, he and writer A.E. Hotchner created a company to sell Newman's homemade salad dressing. The profits were given to charity. Over the years, Newman's company has expanded its product line and it now sells spaghetti sauce, popcorn, steak sauce, salsa, and lemonade. So far, every cent of the $125 million made by the company has gone to charities like the Hole in the Wall Gang Camp in Ashford, Connecticut.[2]

The Hole in the Wall Gang Camp, which takes its name from Newman's film *Butch Cassidy and the Sundance Kid,* provides a respite for children with cancer and other serious illnesses. Newman says that visiting the camp inspires him. The good work being done at those camps should certainly motivate all of us who are blessed with healthy children.

You may not have the time, energy, and resources of a Paul Newman, but you can make a difference. In Boca Raton, Florida, a man who is legally blind has been honored for his charitable endeavors. Thomas Ciulla volunteers at Boca Raton Middle School, tutoring children and performing office work. Despite his handicap, he is doing far more for others than many people whose eyesight is not impaired.[3]

Teachers frequently give back on an ongoing basis. I often see dedicated teachers tutoring students after school so they won't be left behind. Teachers frequently even use their own funds to buy supplies that are missing from their classrooms. It looks like the IRS is finally giving back a little to those teachers who take money out of their own pockets to support their schools. There is now a $250 per year deduction for unreimbursed supplies such as chalk, paper, books, and related computer supplies. It is an above-the-line deduction, which means teachers can utilize it even if they take the standard deduction. It applies to K-12 teachers, as well as aides, counselors, and principals[4].

Even if you don't get a tax deduction, there's nothing to stop you from helping others. Martin Luther King, Jr., said, "You don't have to have a college degree to serve." Reverend King also said, "You don't have to know Einstein's theory of relativity to serve. You only need a heart full of grace and a soul generated by love."[5]

A Message from Garcia

Serve your community. Volunteer your time, energy and resources to charities and other organizations that advocate good causes. Give of yourself selflessly and never expect anything in return. You will derive great personal satisfaction from helping others in this manner. When you give of yourself without expecting anything in return, surprisingly, good things seem to come back to you.

Public service and community involvement help you appreciate your own good fortune. It makes you realize that your view of what constitutes a "tough day" or "bad luck" is nothing when compared to the circumstances faced by some people.

Spending time and energy helping others improves your community and lays the groundwork for future generations. Goodwill is contagious. You will inspire friends and children to do the same and make the world a better place.

CHAPTER 15

··

Success Belief 11:
Be Open to Change

WHEN I WAS A YOUNG LIEUTENANT IN OMAHA, NEBRASKA, I SERVED as an intelligence analyst in a unit that pinpointed signals across the globe to track 10,000 surface-to-air missile sites in countries such as China and what was then the Soviet Union. The location of these missile sites was vitally important since they determined where to deploy our B-52 bombers so they wouldn't be shot down.

Our mission was to account for every missile site and every signal. Each new signal might indicate the presence of a new missile site, which could pose a threat to our country and our allies. When I was first assigned to this unit, I sat down with the men and women who actually did the tracking of signals. I wanted to know how to do their job as well or better than they did. I've never subscribed to the theory that a leader or manager doesn't need to know the work he's overseeing. I always understood the importance of actually doing the work. For the first 60 days of my tenure in Omaha, I worked side by side with the enlisted men and women to appreciate the complexity of their duties.

The job performed by these dedicated men and women was quite tedious. When I first arrived, music was not permitted because the military hierarchy didn't want tape-recording devices in proximity to this extremely sensitive information. I talked the security people into allowing a cassette player that didn't record into the facility so the staff could hear music during their long shifts.

I used the music to motivate the people in my unit. We set up a competition to see who could track the most signals during the week. The person who tracked the most signals was allowed to choose the music for the following week. To listen to the music they loved and to avoid listening to the music they hated, my unit started tracking more signals than they ever had before.

Before I arrived, no one knew how many signals the unit tracked. All that mattered was that the crew worked a full shift, which ran from 5:00 in the afternoon until midnight. Introducing music into the environment helped morale and invigorated everyone's competitive spirit. We worked down the backlog of signals being tracked from 10,000 to 5,000.

I also offered another incentive. When all the "new" signals that came in each day were accounted for, they were allowed to leave for the day, regardless of how much time they had left on their shift. Soon thereafter, these men and women stopped taking breaks, so they could get their work done sooner. Many even began arriving at 2:00 in the afternoon. After a period of 30 days, they worked off the backlog of 5,000 signals.

I received several glowing letters of commendation for working off the backlog. A three-star general even paid us a visit to thank us for our efforts. Regrettably, this general decided to show up at 7:00 P.M. Since all the signals were accounted for, all of us had gone home for the day. The only person present was an unfortunate sergeant who was "holding the fort," a fort missing its workers and filled with electrical equipment! The sergeant had to tell the general that Lieutenant Garcia had let everyone go at 6:00 P.M.

To say the least, the General was not pleased with my initiative. He didn't care that many of the people in my command had come in four hours earlier and had actually completed their assignment for the day. I was called in by my commanding officer, who chewed me out and threatened me with a court-martial. Immediately thereafter, everyone was once again working every minute of every shift, and the number of untracked signals gradually rose upward.

The three-star general did not believe a lieutenant had anything to teach him about managing people. He was not ready for the Garcia version of flextime. At that moment, I realized that I was not meant for the bureaucracy of military life. I longed for private enterprise where you could have accountability for performance and could reward people for achieving common goals. If I was to stay in the military, I knew I would need to find a position where I could be innovative and work with people who were open to change.

Focus on Improving Your Business and Yourself

Even in relatively new companies, certain business practices become ingrained. Instead of scanning the landscape for new opportunities, employees are beating the existing concepts to death, whether or not they seem to work. There was a psychological study done at a racetrack that makes an interesting observation about the decision-making process. In the study, bettors were asked to measure their level of confidence on the way to the betting window. Researchers found that gamblers were only moderately confident in their bet on the way to the window. After they had placed their bet, however, the bettors expressed a higher level of confidence in their choices.[1]

The study concluded that a certain point we all become psychologically attached to the decision that we've made. Once we've made our decision, our mind wants to believe it's correct. In horse racing, however, the horse may finish dead last. When it comes to other decisions, people have a tendency to resist efforts to change their mind.

In business and life, change should be embraced, especially when the status quo isn't working. However, this often is hard to do after you become attached to your decision. The theory of cognitive dissonance suggests that we rely on data that supports our reasoning and defends our position, whereas we choose to ignore facts that disagree with our beliefs and might cause us to have to rethink or change.

In his book *The Leadership Secrets of Colin Powell,* Oren Harari noted that Powell's career has been all about change and that changing things ruffles feathers. Good leaders are constantly asking, "What if?" and "Why not?" They create a culture that demands initiative and experimentation.[2]

Small business experts Paul and Sarah Edwards have offered three suggestions for expanding your business.[3] First, you must determine what your target is. You need to know what you want to accomplish, and when you want to get there. Unless you know what your target is, you can't develop a growth strategy.

The second step is making sure you're ready to grow. Before expanding, every business needs the right infrastructure in place to handle an increased volume of business. More than likely, you'll need a web site, a toll-free number, and the ability to accept all credit cards. You'll probably need more employees as well.

Finally, the Edwards recommended that you figure out what your edge is. What is it that sets your business apart from everyone else's? What assets do you have that the competition doesn't? Those assets will serve as the core of your growth strategy. You must focus on your growth strategy every day of the week. You should revise and improve it if the strategy isn't working as well as you thought it would.

In our personal lives, we often encounter people who would rather do anything but change. They stay in a bad relationship, even though it makes them unhappy. They stay at a bad job, because it's easier than trying to improve their circumstances. These kinds of people rarely focus on improving themselves and their situation. They're resistant to change of any kind, no matter how bad things might be for them at the present time.

Don't Be Afraid to Change Your Personal Beliefs

At a reunion of White House Fellows, I started chatting with the gentleman sitting next to me on the chartered bus. We promptly got into a lively discussion about religion. At that point in my life,

I had taken some religion courses and for a variety of reasons was becoming increasingly disenchanted with Catholicism. As the bus weaved its way through the city, I found myself agreeing 100 percent with my new acquaintance's religious philosophies. As it turned out, this man was a rabbi who was a White House Fellow during a different Presidential administration. We started talking about Judaism, and I found his explanation of Jewish law and philosophy to be refreshing. He told me about Reconstructionism, a type of Judaism.

The conversation triggered my interest in learning more about Judaism. I rapidly found myself reading everything I could find about the religion. Not too long afterward, I learned that my maternal grandmother was Jewish. Later, even before I met my wife, Allison, who is Jewish, I found myself gravitating toward Judaism and several years after we were married converted.

It really didn't matter that the person beside me was a former White House Fellow. I would have engaged that individual in conversation, even if we were on the subway in New York or the bus in a Third World country. Regardless of whom I happen to meet, a rabbi, a former White House Fellow, or a shower curtain salesman, I believe in opening a conversation and starting to learn. Every encounter is an opportunity to grow.

Synchronicity

I believe we are meant to meet certain people who will influence our lives, for a brief moment or for a lifetime. Deepak Chopra defines synchronicity as "a coming together of seemingly unconnected events." According to Chopra, our life is shaped by those moments of meaningful coincidence. And the more we increase our awareness of these moments, the more they happen.[4] Chopra says that by "intending to create synchronicity in your life, you can nurture the result."[5] By cultivating an attitude of relaxed attention and intention, we fulfill what Chopra calls our "SynchroDestiny."

Every chance encounter can have meaning. We learn from the people we meet and our life spins off in a different direction. All these experiences have the potential to help us pursue our dreams. For this to happen, we must consciously work to remain open to transmitting and receiving new information.

Shift Gears Before It's Too Late

If you're open to change, you should be willing to shift gears before it's too late. When we first started Sterling Financial, I hired a computer whiz to design a platform for day trading. I invested a lot of money in the technology. We hoped to partner with one of the largest financial services clearing houses in the world. When we were ready to go after seven months, the firm said it wasn't interested in the platform. This was potentially devastating to our business. We were spending $30,000 to $40,000 per month and no income was in sight. It also didn't help that day trading houses were sprouting up everywhere.

Consequently, I was forced to shift gears. I hired my first broker, who came with a book of business, which means she already had clients who generated income for herself and the firm that employed her. I also shifted our strategy and began focusing on opening offices in Latin America. Shifting gears helped to save a business that was going nowhere. Ultimately, this shift led to a new strategy, which in turn led to our being named as the fastest-growing private company in Florida for two years in a row, 2000 and 2001.

Shifting Gears in Your Personal Life

In our personal lives, we sometimes refuse to shift gears, even when it is obvious we are going nowhere. A child, for example, keeps doing badly in school, but the parents do nothing about it. They don't hire a tutor or spend more time themselves with the child, and the situation continues to get worse.

Every one of us has a friend or relative who drifts from job to job without ever finding success. Even though the person is bright and competent, everywhere he or she goes there are problems. We counsel that friend on how to deal with work situations, but he or she never shifts gears. Such individuals seem incapable of changing their course in life, even though it's clear that they consistently go off in the wrong direction. More than likely, these people will go through life believing that it's everyone else's fault for their lack of success, instead of their own.

A Message from Garcia

Successful people don't just *accept* change, they welcome it and seek out ways to do things better. The workplace must be an environment that fosters creativity and innovation. For enhanced efficiency, productivity and profit, you should encourage new ideas and reward innovative solutions.

Change can help you grow, keep you excited and enthusiastic about life, and prevent burnout. If you are the CEO of a company, by being open to change you will be able to attract bright, creative people to your venture and keep them there. When many businesses are booming, they resist change and don't alter their business strategy until a competitor begins encroaching on their market share. These companies are not proactive but instead wait until the others take the lead before they recognize that they must operate differently in order to remain competitive.

People who get stuck in a rut in their life often resist any possibility or suggestion of change. They continue to bang their head against the same wall and then wonder why they still get the same results. If you're not achieving the success you feel you deserve, it's time for you to change rather than expect the world to. It's never too late to shift gears, and it's often the change you make that will get your career and your personal life moving in the right direction.

CHAPTER 16

....

Success Belief 12:
There Are Many Roads
to Success

WHEN I WAS IN LAW SCHOOL AT COLUMBIA UNIVERSITY, I WAS extremely disappointed that I didn't make the cut as one of the editors of the *Columbia Law Review*. Only 40 students are invited to join the "law review", and I didn't make the cut. The students who make law review usually get prestigious clerkships with judges.

To ease my disappointment, I directed my energies toward Moot Court, which is as close as law students get to the real-world practice of law. Moot Court is a competition in which you analyze a case, draft a brief in support of your position, and present an oral argument to judges who volunteer their time. In the long run, I ended up turning that brief into a law review article. After countless rewrites, the law review editorial board decided to publish my article. I didn't make the law review, but I did manage to get an article published before the students on the law review did. I took a different road, not by choice but by necessity, to achieve my goal.

While successful people look for alternate routes, unsuccessful people put away the map or turn their car around when they think they've reached the end of the road. Instead, they should look for different routes and follow the detours that can often lead to the final destination they are pursuing.

Seek Success In Everything You Do, Even If It Looks Like You Might Fail

There are different roads to success, and the first route you take may not always be the one that gets you there. Michael Jordan was cut from his basketball team in junior high school. To remain involved however, he became the team manager so he could continue to practice with the guys and develop his skills.[1] We all know what happened to him after that.

Tom Clancy, now a very successful author, was an accomplished insurance agent before he began to pursue his passion. Clancy left his secure career in the insurance field and began writing high-tech thrillers. Today, Clancy has numerous best sellers to his credit, and has achieved more success as an author than he ever could have imagined.

Dr. Carole Kanchier advises that you can change your attitude about success. She suggests that you must maintain harmony between who you are and what you do. As your personality evolves, your career must evolve as well. Work rewards should be judged in terms of satisfaction, not money or prestige.[2]

Legendary UCLA basketball coach John Wooden defines success as peace of mind derived from knowing you made the effort to do the best of which you are capable. Wooden recognizes that we are all not equal in talent, but we can make the most of what we have and try to improve at all times.[3]

The Long and Winding Roads to Success

It's not uncommon for entrepreneurs to use the fortune they make in one field to pursue their passion in another industry. Internet billionaire Mark Cuban bought the Dallas Mavericks and spends millions each year trying to win an NBA championship. The eccentric owner worked in a deli growing up, and dreamed of playing professional basketball.

Many entrepreneurs find the movie industry more exciting than their own business, so they finance films as a way to satisfy their interest. Paul Allen, cofounder of Microsoft, invested $500 million in Steven Spielberg's DreamWorks studio. Entrepreneurs such as Michael Bloomberg of Bloomberg, Frederick Smith of FedEx, and Norman Watt of Gateway Computers have all tried their hand at the film-making business.[4]

Napoleon Hill said in *Think And Grow Rich* that one of the most common causes of failure is giving up when you're overtaken by a temporary defeat. Five hundred of the most successful people in the world told Hill that their success came just one step after they thought they were defeated. According to Hill, "Success is a trickster with a keen sense of irony and cunning. It takes great delight in tripping one when success is almost within reach."[5]

What if Sir Laurence Olivier gave up on his dream of being an actor? Greta Garbo demanded that Olivier be fired from a movie in which they were starring. Soon thereafter, a play Olivier was in closed after a week. According to Donald Soto, author of *Laurence Olivier: A Biography*, Olivier thought he was washed up, but he went on to win three Oscars.[6] A Goldwyn talent scout didn't think much of Fred Astaire, either. The scout observed, "Can't act. Can't sing. Slightly bald. Can dance a little."[7] Fortunately, neither Olivier nor Astaire let go of their dreams prematurely.

Success Is Far More than Money and Fame

Success is much more than making money and means different things to different people. Mike Krzyzewski, the head coach of Duke's very successful basketball team, wrote this about his mother. "I think of my mom every day of my life. She was as happy a person as I've ever been around. She made fun of herself and was telling jokes until the day she died—literally. She never had much money. No cars. She didn't have a house. But she was happy. She led a great life. She was proud. And people loved her. Tell me that's not success," Coach K wrote.[8]

My own mother was an incredible success. She gave up a promising career in medicine to marry my father. She adjusted to life in a foreign country and took up a new career, teaching science to seventh graders. My mother was beloved by her students, and she had an enormously positive impact on their lives.

A Message from Garcia

Once you understand your greatest strengths and what your goals in life are, then you must concentrate all your energy into making them a reality. During your journey to success, consider adopting the fourteen *Success Beliefs* as the lenses through which you view the world. Once you know where you are going and have the necessary belief structure to attract success, you need a clear and well-defined strategy. The four *Success Strategies,* discussed later in the book, will provide you with a blueprint of the essential action steps to employ in the pursuit of your dreams.

People who have achieved success know through trial and error, through failure and perseverance, that there is more than one road to success. No matter how many times you get knocked off your horse, pick yourself up and get back in the saddle. If you keep learning from every setback, you'll eventually get there. Keep your eyes on the prize and be ready to change your plans if necessary. Be flexible and adaptable to situations. Be prepared to modify your approach as necessary. Remain focused on the goal, but be resilient and remain vigilant in the pursuit of the ultimate objective. Adapt to whatever situation arises. Be ingenious and discover the many hidden ways to your goal. And if there seems to be none, make one up!

CHAPTER 17

Success Belief 13: Successful People Are Tenacious

IN THE TELEVISION MOVIE "DOOR TO DOOR," ACTOR WILLIAM H. Macy plays Bill Porter, a victim of cerebral palsy. Porter did not let his medical condition stop him from becoming one of the best door-to-door salesmen. Even after being told repeatedly that he was unemployable, he never gave up his dream of finding a job. Porter finally convinced the Watkins Company to give him a chance to sell household goods door to door. Although his medical problem slurred his speech and made it difficult for him to walk, Porter worked harder than anyone to become a successful salesman. Despite debilitating back pain, migraines, and arthritis, Porter became Watkins' number one salesman in his territory for more than 10 years.

Frequently, Porter was told to give up his dream and accept disability benefits, but he would not listen. Urged by his mother, he followed in the footsteps of his late father, who had been an exceptional salesman. Porter became a fixture in his rundown Portland, Oregon, neighborhood. To keep him going in the face of ridicule and rejection, his mother would leave him inspirational messages in the oddest places, including the sandwiches she would make him for lunch. On one side of the sandwich, she wrote a note that read "patience"; if you flipped it over, the other side read "persistence." Bill Porter gobbled up his lunches and did more than digest these principles. He made them a part of his being. Porter became Watkins' number one salesperson in California, Idaho, Oregon, and Washington.[1]

Much like Bill Porter, a young man named Jaime Gonzalez has been dealing with difficult circumstances since birth, yet he continues to move closer to achieving his dream of being a doctor. Gonzalez, a young Hispanic boy, wasn't expected to live to see his first birthday. He also wasn't expected to walk because of serious birth defects. His mother disagreed and took him for daily physical therapy sessions, refusing to confine him to a wheelchair. For years, Gonzalez took a bus for the physically disabled to magnet classes. Gonzalez arrived home at 4:00 P.M. and went from there to his part-time job at the local community center, working from 5:00 until 9:00. His grade-point average was 4.2 and he was recruited by almost all of the top schools in the country.

Gonzalez's father, a sample cutter in the garment district, wanted the best education for his son, even though he personally had to drop out of school in the fourth grade. His mother, a part-time cafeteria worker, taught him that he could do anything and there are no obstacles that can't be overcome. They never let him feel sorry for himself. His parents motivated him and treated him the same as his younger brother. The years of hard work are paying off for Gonzalez. His dream of becoming a doctor is within reach after winning a four-year scholarship to an undergraduate premed program at the University of Southern California and another four-year scholarship for medical school.[2]

A tumultuous side trip to Southeast Asia almost derailed Rocky Bleier's dream of playing professional football. An undersized running back, he was drafted in a very late round by the Pittsburgh Steelers in 1968. Although he was a great college player at Notre Dame, Bleier did not appear to have what it took to play professional football. Before making his mark with the Steelers, Bleier was drafted again, only this time it was the army who came calling.

Within a few months, far from the playing fields of the National Football League, Bleier was wounded in Vietnam. He returned to the states, barely able to walk, let alone run plays on a football field. For two years, he struggled to regain the skills that would allow him to play professional football. Four years later, Bleier ran a faster 40-yard dash than he ever had. Because of his tenacity and courage, Bleier returned to his former profession. He was a starter on the Steelers' four Super Bowl teams and passed the 1,000-yard rushing mark one season.

Jim Abbott became a successful major league pitcher, despite being born without a right hand. As a youngster, Abbott learned to throw and catch a baseball with one hand by bouncing the ball against the wall for hours. He was the winning pitcher for the United States at the 1988 Olympics when the American team beat Japan for the gold medal. As a professional baseball player, Abbott pitched a no-hitter for the Yankees in 1993 against the Cleveland Indians.

People with disabilities are often the most tenacious, because they must work even harder to achieve success. Dan Andrews, a student at the University of Miami, is the only amputee competing in NCAA Division I track meets. These are not the Para-Olympics events that Andrews wins with regularity; he races against other college athletes who do not have a disability. Andrews broke his shinbone in a soccer accident in 1996 and suffered complications that led to oxygen deprivation in his lower leg. Doctors were forced to amputate his leg just below the knee. Within six months, Andrews was back on the soccer field as a goalie and six months later he was running using a carbon-fiber artificial leg.[3]

A walk-on football player tried out for the Penn State team in August 2002. The player was told to give up football because of reconstructive knee surgery. Yet she is still trying to make the team, despite years of being told she wasn't good enough to kick for an all-male football team. Stephanie Weimer has proved skeptics wrong in the past. During her senior year, she kicked more field goals than any other high school player in her division. Her career highlights included a 36-yard field goal, as well as a touch-down-saving tackle. She may never play for Joe Paterno's Penn State team, but she hasn't let her sex or her injury stand in the way of pursuing her dream.[4]

A Message from Garcia

Determination and tenacity are essential character traits to help you reach your goals. Having the skills, knowledge and talent is important, but achieving your dream is possible only when you are tenacious. Regardless of what others think, prove them wrong by sticking to it and doing what it takes to accomplish whatever it is you are setting out to do.

Develop the tools and the character to deal with the curveballs that life will throw your way. Rocky Bleier and Jim Abbott were both thrown vicious curveballs and managed to catch them with one hand. Like other successful people, they possessed the tenacity and the character to play the hand they were dealt. Not only did they make the best of it, they also achieved tremendous success despite their challenges.

Having a dream is good. But having a dream and doing something about it is better. Be creative and resourceful in your efforts to achieve your goals. Above all else, start acting instead of procrastinating. People spend an enormous amount of time and energy just talking about what they want or what they are going to do. If you want to achieve something, do as the Nike television commercial says and "Just do it."

Success Belief 14: Cultivate Business and Personal Relationships

AN EXCELLENT WAY TO ACHIEVE BALANCE IN YOUR LIFE IS BY friendships. I always appreciated the camaraderie of law school. I found that too many students were overly competitive and missed out on the many friendships they might have enjoyed. I still have friends from my days at the Air Force Academy, law school, from my time at the White House, and from my military service. The relationships made in the military are particularly strong. These are people you may go to war with, and the bond that develops may be tested on the battlefield.

Building and maintaining a great relationship with someone is one of the most important and rewarding aspects of life. Those relationships can help you deal with adversity. They give you a pool of people to call on for advice and counsel.

Relationships Can Change Your Life

We've all heard the expression "It's not what you know, but who you know." And quite frankly, there is a great deal of truth to that expression. As Oriental wisdom teaches, in my case discovered from reading a fortune cookie some years ago: A wise man knows everything; a shrewd man knows everyone. Of course, having smarts counts, whether it's book smarts and a good education, or being bright, street-smart and savvy. Regardless of your intelligence and how you came by it, Keith Ferrazzi has elevated that famous expression to a new level.

Keith Ferrazzi, the 36-year-old CEO of Los Angles-based YaYa, a video game creator, makes knowing the right people and creating relationships through the mastery of networking the cornerstone of his being. Ferrazzi has achieved exceptional success through his passion for cultivating relationships. In other words, Ferrazzi is passionate about networking so much so that you could say that he has networking *ganas*. I decided to meet Ferrazzi after reading about his networking skills in a feature story in the December 2002 issue of *Inc* magazine.

Like all people who achieve extraordinary success in a particular field, rising to the top of their game due to natural born talent, Ferrazzi likewise seemed to have an innate talent in the arena of networking and relationship building. I was so intrigued by Ferrazzi's mastery of networking and the value he puts on relationships that I tracked him down to discuss his views on the subject.

After catching up to him at the Yale Club in New York City, where Ferrazzi lunches regularly, I asked him when he began to develop his networking techniques, and Ferrazzi revealed to me that he recalls his first true networking experience when he was in fourth grade. "One of my friends had a father who was a lawyer who was kind of getting into politics," said Ferrazzi, "and I remember that I wanted to get to know him. He was a lawyer, and I didn't know any lawyers. My father was blue collar, my family was blue collar, and we had blue collar friends." When I asked why he thought it was important to get to know him, Ferrazzi said that he wanted to reach up, he wanted to "be on the radar screen of this man who Ferrazzi thought was going places and Ferrazzi wanted him to know Ferrazzi was a bright young man."

That was then, this is now. Ferrazzi has reached up, all the way up. Today, at the age of 36, Ferrazzi has not only reached up, but he touches those at the highest levels of business, government, politics, and media. Take, for instance, Michael Milken—Ferrazzi knows him. Barry Diller? Ferrazzi knows him. Former President Bill Clinton? Ferrazzi knows him, too.

Ferrazzi believes that business is a bit of a game. And the rule in the game that trumps all others, Ferrazzi became convinced, is that those that combine hard work, thoughtful insights and deep broad relationships become members of the club, not the caddy. Ferrazzi didn't stumble upon that theory, but came upon it honestly while a youngster by lugging around the golf clubs of the rich and powerful at a country club where he caddied. It's been a long time since Ferrazzi has hauled anyone's golf clubs around and now people want to know him. His firm, YaYa, has captured more than its fair share of attention, due in part to Ferrazzi's prized relationships with the media and some of the world's most powerful journalists.

But before networking his way to the presidency of YaYa, Ferrazzi cultivated relationships that yielded an extraordinary resume that reads like the classic rags-to-riches American success story. A poor kid born to a steel worker and a cleaning lady, Ferrazzi's father had the gumption to ask his boss's boss to meet the young Ferrazzi. "My father wanted a better life for me," says Ferrazzi "and he knew that the only way I could do it was by getting a better education." Ferrazzi's father was successful in establishing that connection for his son, and the younger Ferrazzi made the right impression and the right moves with the right people and got into a prestigious elementary school. Through those connections Ferrazzi went on to receive the best education available in America. After graduating from an elite prep school then Yale, he went to Harvard Business School. Ferrazzi then became the youngest nominated partner at Deloitte Consulting, and later, then the youngest Fortune 500 chief marketing officer, by working at Starwood Hotels. He then got tapped by famed financier Michael Milken to become CEO of YaYa, a pioneering company in the creation of on-line games as custom marketing vehicles.

After being shadowed for nearly six months by a reporter for the *Inc.* article, Ferrazzi's key networking theories were reduced to the following 10 secrets:

Rule 1. Don't network just to network. Know what you want from the relationship and go after it.

Rule 2. Take Names. If you see the name of someone you want to know, or think you want to know, keep it somewhere and find a reason and a way to contact that person at some point.

Rule 3. Build it before you need it. Have your network in place, cultivate it, and be sure your relationships are secure, and have provided value to those with whom you are in a relationship before you actually ask them for something.

Rule 4. Never eat alone. Keep a high public profile, keep your social calendar full.

Rule 5. Be interesting. Look different, be different, have something smart to say, read the newspaper, and make people want to talk to you and know you.

Rule 6. Manage the gatekeeper artfully. Learn the art and craft of managing or influencing secretaries. They control the access to those to whom you need or want to speak.

Rule 7. Always ask. Ask for what you want. It never hurts to ask; the worst anyone can do is say no. Not many people believe that; embarrassment and fear are debilitating.

Rule 8. Don't keep score. Successful networking is never about simply getting what you want. It's first about making sure that people who are important to you get what they want.

Rule 9. Ping constantly. Eighty percent of networking is just staying in touch. Find any and every reason to stay in touch with people.

Rule 10. Find anchor tenants, and then feed them. Always be on the lookout for people one or two levels above you and find reasons to invite them to an event, such as a dinner, a lunch, a breakfast, where they join something and also become "the anchor" that is intriguing and interesting to others.

I asked Ferrazzi what advice he would give to someone who was just starting out to try and develop their own networking skills. He suggested starting small. Just start reaching up and out. Spread the word with people you know, and try to create a group of interesting people that might be of interest to other interesting people who are above your present social and economic status.

As a final note, Ferrazzi points out that networking is about giving and the first and foremost benefit from networking is the joy of giving. "My objective when putting people together is not to take something from the outcome of having put two people together, but rather do it for the joy that I get from having put two people together." This is the quid pro quo.

Find a Mentor

I've already stressed that to pursue your passions, you need to find a mentor who's already in the field that interests you. With that relationship, you can build a career in a field that excites you, rather than just going to work each day to a job that gives you no personal satisfaction.

This lesson was brought home to me by one of my closest mentors, Seymour Holtzman, who made a habit of solving tough problems by calling upon business people with whom he had relationships. Holtzman would reach out to friends with as much knowledge about the subject as him or others who were experts in the field in which he needed counsel. He would call upon these people if a difficult problem arose and they would provide advice.

Holtzman would test ideas and run his thoughts by them. In turn, if those people needed advice with specific situations, Holtzman was a phone call away. Their advice was impartial and objective because they were viewing the situation from afar. It didn't matter what day of the week it was, if he had a problem and needed to resolve it, he would reach out day or night to relationships for their advice. Once he got what he was seeking, he made the best possible decision in the light of all of the information. He moved forward with a confidence that inspired everyone around him. Someone once described Seymour this way: "Sometimes wrong, but never in doubt." Entrepreneurs are not always right, but sometimes you achieve success by going confidently down a path, without doubt and without fear.

Tap Into Personal Relationships for Wise Advice

Learning from my experience with Holtzman, I pick up the phone whenever major issues concern me. I'll run the situation and my ideas for resolving it past a number of people who are much smarter than me. I respect the opinions of these people, and they always seem to steer me in the right direction. Likewise, I am here for these individuals when they need me.

It is important for entrepreneurs and business people to cultivate relationships with individuals who can be called on for smart, third party, impartial advice. I work with a group in Florida called TEC, which stands for The Executive Committee. It is a group of former Fortune 1000 executives who give advice to entrepreneurs, and a group of 10 to 14 CEOs that get together once a month to discuss problems and look for solutions. I've also joined a program sponsored by the Florida Chamber of Commerce called Leadership Florida, which provides access to a group of smart, experienced leaders from across the state who can offer valuable advice to members like myself. The Young President's Organization, or YPO, is another excellent organization that I belong to. YPO consists of a group of talented young CEOs that provide friendly advice and valuable help when you need it.

Even if you're not in business for yourself, it pays to cultivate relationships with your coworkers. In every type of business, you need mentors and people whom you can bounce ideas off when necessary. Your chances of success at work improve if you establish good relationships with coworkers. You're viewed as a team player, not a lone wolf. You build bridges with different people and different departments, instead of isolating yourself.

Never rely on only one opinion, whether it's a business matter or a personal one. If you have a heart problem, consult with three of the best cardiologists, not just one. Similarly, if you have a tax problem, consult with three experienced accountants. If it's a legal issue, discuss it with at least three lawyers. Different professionals have different experiences and can offer different advice about the same problem.

In your own family, there are people who can advise you on all types of issues. Of course, there are personal or business matters that don't always need to be shared, but there might be members of your family who can offer objective advice on any number of issues you might face. If someone in your family has achieved the kind of success you're looking for, or even success in a different field, you can draw upon some of that knowledge to aid you in your own life.

Think about your family and friends, and write down which ones have expertise in particular areas. When you run into a problem, don't be afraid to give them a call and tap into their expertise. Asking advice in business is not much different from the kind of feedback we often seek when shopping for a car; we have a tendency to ask everyone what they think, how they like it, what they may have heard, etc. Along with our own research, we seem to always ask friends and family for their opinions about which make and model to buy.

Smart and successful people are willing to admit they need additional knowledge to help make certain decisions. It's the ones who think they know everything who don't tap into the intelligence of others.

The Message from Garcia

Being smart is good. Being smart and knowing a lot of smart people is better. Networking is essential to achieving great success. Successful people know and interact with other successful people. Successful people cultivate and nurture these relationships to enhance their personal and business lives. Try to meet others in your fields who are above you, people who are well known and who have excellent reputations. Meet people from outside your field. By interacting with people outside your immediate field, you increase your network of relationships. These people can bring a fresh perspective to your personal and business life and you can likewise offer the same to them. Be interesting, informative and willing to help others without expecting to earn something in return.

By having a wide network of relationships, you can solicit the opinions of others to get their take on a problem or situation you might be facing. Third-party, impartial advice can be valuable. When no one has a stake in a decision or an emotional connection to it, their perspective can be clearer and often more valid. When faced with a particularly demanding problem, reach into your network for more than one opinion from people whom you respect. By getting at least three opinions on any one matter you should be able to decipher the correct course of action.

PART THREE

SUCCESS STRATEGY 1: DREAM BIG

CHAPTER 19

....

The Four
Success Strategies:
Dream Big,
Start Planning Now,
Take Action,
and Persevere

YOU WANT TO BE SUCCESSFUL. YOU BOUGHT THIS BOOK. NOW, ALL you need is a realistic strategy to achieve those dreams. First of all, your dream has to be clear and well defined. It cannot be, "I want to make more money or "I want to get rich." Those are goals, but what you need is a strategy to achieve them. The rest of this book will offer specific strategies to achieve success. It will show you how to plan your life with the goal of achieving your dreams.

Let's face it, almost everyone wants to get rich, and to get rich *now*. What's more, you want to get rich without working hard for it. There are two ways this can happen—win the lottery or invest in Internet and hi-tech companies during the late 1990s. Here's the bad news: you missed the 1990s, and your chances of winning the lottery are something like 1 in 30 million. Most other solutions will require a bit more motivation. If you're willing to work hard to achieve success, there's a much better chance than 1 in 30 million that you will achieve it.

In addition to the 14 "Success Beliefs" described earlier, here are four success strategies:

1. Dream big.
2. Start planning now.
3. Take immediate action.
4. Persevere.

These strategies are simple, and that's precisely why they work. Often in life, the answers to difficult questions are right in front of us. The solutions are simple, but we keep trying to complicate matters or choose to ignore the obvious answer.

I have discovered that successful people follow simple time-tested strategies, and practice them over and over again until they perfect them. Legendary football coach Vince Lombardi is a perfect example. From 1959 to 1967, Coach Lombardi turned a perpetual loser, the Green Bay Packers, into national champions.

Before the start of his first season, Lombardi preached the following message to his team: "The good Lord gave you a body that can stand most anything. It's your mind you have to convince." His philosophy was to focus on the fundamentals and drill them into his players over and over, until they were doing it the right way. Coach Lombardi proved that repetition builds confidence, and confidence builds passion. Repetition, confidence, and passion were the three pillars of Lombardi's football success, and the secret to Lombardi's coaching success was his philosophy that perfection came with simplicity. He rejected the many fads and new football techniques in vogue during his era, and distilled the game into the basic fundamentals.

Lombardi and the Green Bay Packers went on to win the first two Super Bowls and three other NFL championships. In the process, Lombardi became the NFL coach with the best win/loss record, with a percentage of .740 (105-35-6). He was so successful that the NFL named its 10-pound, handcrafted sterling silver Tiffany Super Bowl trophy the Lombardi Trophy.

Success can be defined in simple strategies: committing to your dream, developing a realistic plan, taking action, and persevering until your dreams become a reality. Follow these strategies and you will succeed.

Action Strategy 1: Dream Big

The first of these strategies is to dream big. When I say, "dream big," I mean, dream *big*! Push reality aside for the moment and think about anything and everything that you could possibly want out of life. Remember, it is important that you are doing this exercise "after" you have read *Now, Discover Your Strengths* and taken the Emode test in Chapter 3. And remember to write down your dreams on paper. Go to *www.successcompass.com* and fill out your *Success Compass*™ today!

Action Strategy 2: Start Planning Now

Unfortunately, most people go through life without a flight plan for success, going day to day without an overall vision that will get them from where they are now to where they want to be. They head off in a direction chosen at random, with no clear picture of where they want to be in 1 year, 5 years, or 10 years. Having no strategy often leaves them grounded in an unrewarding career and quite possibly a life that seems unfulfilled.

Every successful company has a business plan. The business plan sets forth the company's mission, its guiding principles, and its strategy for making money. Like a flight plan, the business plan articulates the direction in which the company is headed and how it intends to get there.

Action Strategy 3: Take Action

How many times have you, or someone you know, talked about a great idea, about a desire to change jobs, start a new career, take a course, or even go back to school to get that high school diploma, college degree, or master's degree that slipped through your hands? It might have been an urge to take an art course or learn martial arts, fencing, photography, or bridge, or any one of a million things we so often become inspired to achieve on a whim. Every single day across this country a million people get a million great ideas, or have urges or desires to do something exciting. The difference between people who are successful and those who are not is in that one step, that one leap, that one critical moment when one stops thinking and talking about something, and actually starts doing it.

One of the most brilliant television campaigns ever created was by Nike, consisting of three simple words that capitalized on the difference between being fit or flabby, between losing weight or just jabbering about it—"Just do it." This compelling campaign has helped in the shaping and firming of America, and resulted in tremendous sales for Nike. That, my friends, is the key to almost anything; stop talking about something and just do it.

Action Strategy 4: Persevere

Failure is just a steppingstone to success. Oprah Winfrey was fired from her reporter's job, but instead of quitting, she learned from her mistakes and went on to become one of the most loved and successful women in television. Elvis Presley was fired from the Grand Ole Opry after only one performance. The manager said, "You ain't goin' nowhere, son. Better get y'all a job back driving a truck." Even Walter Cronkite, America's most recognized and respected voice on television, failed an early audition in local radio; the station manager told him that he would *never* succeed as a radio announcer!

Your life is a process, a process made up of thousands of experiences molding who you are today. All of those experiences, including all the mistakes or temporary setbacks, are just incredible opportunities God has given you to strike out in a different direction. When promising young soccer star Julio Iglesias was in a terrible car accident, he thought his life was over. After 14 hours of surgery, he was left paralyzed. Doctors predicted he would never walk again. During an extraordinary three-year recuperation period while he learned to walk again, Iglesias passed the time and kept back his depression over his failed life by strumming on a guitar given to him by a physician's assistant. Iglesias continued to play the guitar, focused on his music, and went on to become one of the world's most successful recording artists.

You will notice that this book is a manual, a reference guide to becoming successful. There is no one secret ingredient. All components must be present to yield success. The concept of perseverance is as essential as the other key ingredients discussed in this book.

Perseverance is indeed a prominent quality in all highly successful people. Some call it determination, other call it stick-to-itiveness. Whatever you choose to call it, know this: if you want something really bad, you must have the commitment to pursue it through thick and thin, through all the tough times, through the negativity you will receive from those who will try to persuade you to give up, or do something else. What is failure? Nothing but an education, merely the first step on to something better. Never give up, never give in. If you have but an ounce of talent and brains, you will eventually succeed, as long as you do not quit. As you may have frequently heard, the line between success and failure is so thin, we often don't realize when we have crossed it.

A Message from Garcia

If you want to achieve great success you must have a clear picture of the goal in mind and a strategy to achieve that goal. A goal without a strategy is like a plane without a flight plan. You know where you want to go; now you need to know how to get there. In addition to the 14 Success Beliefs, you need to employ 4 Success Strategies: Dream Big, Start Planning Now, Take Action, Persevere. These strategies will help you get to your final destination—success, whatever it is that it may be for you. Be prepared for a long, hard journey. Nothing worth accomplishing is ever easy. Never quit, and do not let others dissuade you from pursuing your dream.

Write down your dreams on a piece of paper and carry it with you at all times. Use the *Success Compass*™ program (free) that I developed to facilitate the process of crystallizing your thoughts into writing. Visualize the type of person you want to be and commit yourself to the process of achieving your goals. Remain alert, keeping eyes and ears open to anything and everything that will provide wood for the fire of your dream. Do not allow anything to undermine your determination. Wake up every morning knowing that what you want to achieve is one step closer. What you're doing is creating a business plan for your life.

CHAPTER 20

Pursue Your Dreams

LIFE CAN BE LIKE STANDING AT THE BASE OF MOUNT EVEREST. YOU can face the challenge and choose to climb it, or you can walk around it. Those who climb it see sights that few others ever see, and earn an achievement that few ever know. Daniel Ruettiger was a young man when he chose to climb his metaphorical mountain.

By all accounts, Ruettiger was not destined for success. Born in Jolliet, Illinois in 1948, Ruettiger was the third child in a family of 14. As you might expect, his family was poor. His father worked in an oil refinery. Ruettiger himself was short, 5 feet, 6 inches, and by all accounts not that smart. Later in his life it was discovered that he had a mild form of dyslexia, which explains his poor school performance. It seems Ruettiger was destined for a life of sameness, not greatness. But Ruettiger inherited his father's passion for the Notre Dame football team. As a youngster Ruettiger often would announce his intention to go to Notre Dame and play for the fighting Irish.

After a stint in the Navy, he returned to the power plant where he thought he would complete his life. Then, something unexpected happened. At the plant, Ruettiger's best friend was killed in an industrial accident. The incident rekindled his childhood dream, his passion to go to Notre Dame and play on the football team. The idea was crazy. Ruettiger did not have the talent, the brains, or the money to go to Notre Dame, but this did not stop him.

The first thing he did was to go to South Bend. He knew he did not have the grades or the money to get into Notre Dame, but according to his own game plan, Ruettiger did the next best thing. He got a job working in the gym where the Notre Dame football athletes trained. Ruettiger did not have the money for his own place, but a sympathetic field worker arranged it so that Ruettiger could sleep on a cot at the gym. He enrolled at Holy Cross College across the street from Notre Dame, where an understanding priest acted as a mentor.

After two years of living this way and various attempts to gain admission to Notre Dame, Ruettiger was finally accepted. Once accepted, Ruettiger tried out for the Notre Dame football team as a walk-on. Not good enough to start or to even substitute, Ruettiger volunteered to be part of the practice team against whom the starting bruisers would play regularly during practice. Gigantic athletes literally twice the size of Ruettiger would punish him day in and day out. Ruettiger subjected himself to this physical and mental abuse for two years, all while holding on to the dream of simply being able to suit up and play in even one play for Notre Dame. There were times when he wanted to quit, but in Ruettiger's mind, quitting was not an option. Ruettiger wanted to be part of his dream team even for just one play.

On the last play of the season during the year in which Ruettiger was going to graduate, he finally got his chance. With 27 seconds on the clock and when his teammates, whose hearts and spirit Ruettiger had captured, threatened to walk off the field if he did not play, the coach put Ruettiger in for the last play of the game. During these last few seconds, Ruettiger sacked the opposing team's quarterback. Ruettiger is the only player in the school's history to be carried off the field on his teammate's shoulders. He graduated from Notre Dame with honors and paved the way for five of his younger siblings to attend and graduate from Notre Dame.

Ruettiger's story was turned into the hit movie *Rudy* in 1993. The film was the first to be shot on the Notre Dame campus since *Knute Rockne, All American* in 1940. After the release of the film, Ruettiger went on to become an international celebrity, as well as an acclaimed motivational speaker and author, sharing the speaking platform with many great leaders and speakers. When Rudy was asked why he wanted to make the team so badly, he said, "this is for everyone who told me that I couldn't do it."

Reevaluating Your Life

Earlier in this book I gave some examples of people doing what others wanted them to do before finally coming around to doing what they really wanted to do. Theresa Park is a woman who succumbed to her family's wishes that she become a successful professional before doing anything that she might desire. Theresa had an extraordinary childhood. Her father worked for the United Nations and Theresa grew up in places like Germany, Lebanon, and Austria. In large part to fulfill her family's wishes, she decided to go to Harvard Law School and pursue a legal career. Her international experience and her desire to work in the human rights arena led her to spend her summers in some interesting places, with human rights groups in Uganda and Turkey.

During her last semester at Harvard, Theresa decided that the best way to pay off her mounting law school loans was to take a job as a high-powered corporate lawyer. She moved to Palo Alto, California, to work for one of the most prestigious law firms in the country. Theresa did this for 15 months, but despite the money, the prestige, the privilege, and the potential that accompanied this post, she felt unfulfilled and unsatisfied.

Theresa reevaluated her life and her career path. As an undergraduate student at the University of California, Santa Cruz, she double-majored in political science and creative writing. Something about writing appealed to her but not as a writer per se. She thought she might like the field of publishing. After her husband decided to accept a job at a law firm in New York City, she decided to seriously explore the possibility of becoming a literary agent instead of finding a job at a law firm in New York.

Literary agents are the conduits between an author, or aspiring author, and the book publishing companies. They are, in a manner of speaking, brokers. They try to find new authors whose works they feel are worthy of being published. This appealed to her because it would allow her to use the negotiating and contractual skills she developed as a lawyer, as well as tap into her creative writing talents. Many literary agents play an active role in providing editing and direction on the initial work to bring it up to the level that the agent thinks will make it the best work possible and to increase the chances of the work being accepted by a publisher. This was a good field for Theresa.

The best book agents in the country are in Los Angeles and New York— Los Angeles mostly for screenplay agents, New York for the book publishing and literary worlds. Theresa was moving to New York, and book publishing it would be. She knew no one, and had no mentor. Her first step was to learn about the industry. She purchased a book, *The Complete Guide to Literary Agents*, and learned the basics. Then, she started calling the top 100 book agents in the city. Over a period of several weeks she cold-called virtually every literary agency in New York. According to Theresa, it was depressing. "No one would talk to me," she says. But the people that did talk to Theresa were mainly the assistants. "Most of the shops consist of one to three people," says Theresa, "I was able to extract nuggets of information from different assistants and eventually quilted together a greater knowledge of the business, the people, who did what, and how things got done."

Theresa was undeterred. The more she learned, despite the challenges and obstacles of breaking into a closed industry, the more fascinating she found it and began to really believe that this was something she wanted to do. She prepared her résumé and began sending it out. She followed up with a new round of phone calls. Eventually, her persistence paid off and she got an interview.

At one firm, there were two agents who needed a full-time assistant. The two agents were women. "I immediately connected with them," says Theresa, "I think they saw how passionate I was about wanting to be in the business. After all, I was making a major financial sacrifice to get my foot in the door." The salary was only $18,000. Remember, Theresa was a Harvard trained lawyer, and her former secretary in Palo Alto would be making twice as much as Theresa's new salary. But, her heart wasn't in law, and Theresa was willing to make the sacrifice for something she was passionate about. She wanted to be a literary agent so she accepted the job at Sanford Greenburger Associates. However, she negotiated her deal so that she had the right to seek out her own authors without having to wait the traditional two-year period of apprenticing in the business.

Theresa would work all day and then around 6:00 P.M., she'd rummage through what's called the *slush pile*, where all the submitted query letters and manuscripts go that have been "passed on". Query letters are the initial letters of introduction sent by authors to the agency intended to pique the interest of the agency, describe the story, and provide some background and credentials of the author. Query letters are generally one-page letters. If the agent likes the query letter, the agent will either call the author or write a note on the letter and send it back giving the go-ahead for the author to submit the full manuscript. According to Theresa, "there had to be something in there, and if there was, I knew I would find it."

Theresa spent about a year slogging through the slush pile, but despite the many late nights, nothing really caught her attention. Then, as if Theresa was living her own novel, a dramatic incident occurred. An agent in the office died rather suddenly, and as a result Theresa began to review some of the query submissions that continued to arrive for the deceased agent, which were passed on to her by the agent's former assistant. Finally, Theresa came upon something that caught her attention, a 250-page manuscript about two elderly people in love set in North Carolina in the mid-1940s, an achingly tender story about the enduring power of love. As Theresa said, "It was romantic, it had me in tears, and I knew there had to be something here."

Theresa called the aspiring author, a 28-year old pharmaceutical salesman who had never been published. The manuscript had been rejected by 25 other agents. "I told him it was a diamond in the rough and that it needed a lot of work," says Theresa. She asked him if he would be willing to do rewrites. He said yes. Theresa offered tremendous input, and significant revisions were made by both. When they were both satisfied with the manuscript, they needed a name. That was Theresa's department, and she came up with a title.

Theresa began to do her thing. She put the manuscript out there to different publishing houses, pitching it as the next *Bridges of Madison County*. Jamie Raab at Warner Books bit on it first with an offer of $500,000, which for a first-time author was a big deal. But Theresa, drawing upon her legal skills, refused the first offer, confident that it was a preemptive offer, intended to just tie up the book and get it off the market so no one else would snap it up. Theresa boldly countered that she had a bestseller on her hands and she was looking for a seven-figure deal. Jamie told Theresa that she would get back to her. Now came the waiting game. Would they call or wouldn't they?

Theresa's mentor thought she was nuts for declining. Amazingly, the phone rang barely 10 minutes later. It was Jamie Raab, Warner doubled the offer to $1 million and the deal was done.

The name of the finished book became *The Notebook* and the author was Nicholas Sparks. This first novel by Sparks spent over two years on the bestseller lists in the United States and around the world. Theresa went from slogging through slush piles in the evenings to a comfortable office of her own. She went on to represent Nicholas Sparks in a few more book-to-movie deals on titles that might be familiar to you.

Sparks followed up with *Message in a Bottle* (1998), *A Walk to Remember* (1998), *The Rescue* (2000), *A Bend in the Road* (2001), and *Nights in Rodanthe* (2002). All were domestic and international bestsellers and were translated into more than 35 languages. The movie version of *Message in a Bottle* was released in 1999, and *A Walk to Remember* was released in January 2002. The film version for *The Notebook* will be released in 2003. Jamie Raab went on to become senior vice president and publisher of Warner Books, and Theresa Park went on to become one of the most sought-after literary agents in the business.

Her desire to pursue a career in the literary field was paramount. She sacrificed a great deal and overcame tremendous obstacles along the way, particularly breaking into a field as tight-knit and closed as the one she chose. But she remained undeterred and unfazed. "There are very few things more depressing than going to work every day at a job you hate," says Theresa. Theresa points out that it was hard at the beginning, but "I was doing something I loved and it is better than being miserable."

Theresa is not only happy and successful, but by pursuing her passion she will bring to market authors whose desire to be discovered so that they may pursue their own passion is as challenging to them as to her own journey to success.

Make Time for Success

In his book *Success Is a Journey*, Jeffrey J. Mayer says that successful people give themselves an extra hour each day. When they want to get something done, they'll get up an hour early. As a result, they're able to accomplish something very important before breakfast.[1]

Perhaps you love to paint but never find the time. With that one additional hour, you can put brush to canvas and see where the inspiration takes you. If you dream of writing a screenplay or the great american novel, you will be amazed at how much you can write in just one hour a day. Author Scott Turow wrote his first best-selling novel, *Presumed Innocent*, in longhand while commuting back and forth to his job as a lawyer in Chicago.

Mayer also stresses the importance of making one more phone call or completing one more task before calling it a day. Those phone calls helped his career, as he reached hundreds of people who were still at their desk. Each month you'll make 20 calls you wouldn't have gotten to, or will have completed 20 additional tasks.

How about that lunch hour? Is it spent productively, or do you spend it whining about your boss, coworkers, or customers? Keep moving toward positive goals instead of wasting your energy on the negative aspects of your life.

You'll be in a far better position to reach your goals if you block out time to achieve them. With that extra hour, you'll be focusing your energy on completing a single task. Even if you're a free spirit, a schedule will help you find time for learning and achieving. Now is the time to start making time for what really matters in your life.

A Message from Garcia

If you have a dream, you have a tremendous edge over many people. Most people do not have a dream. If you know exactly what your strengths are, what you want to be, or what you want to do, you are way ahead of other people. Depending upon your age and position in life, pursuing your dream might require great sacrifice. You must be prepared for a great struggle if you want to achieve great levels of success. Only you can determine if it is worth it. Only you can decide if you can get up earlier in the morning to work on something, and make the necessary sacrifices to focus on the achievement of those dreams. People who choose to pursue a dream do so with a passion that overshadows all of the negative consequences that oftentimes result from the challenges and difficulties of achieving great success.

CHAPTER 21

··

Fear Will Hold You Prisoner, and Hope Will Set You Free

NORWEGIAN ADVENTURER THOR HEYERDAHL SEEMED FEARLESS TO all of us who read about his 101-day voyage on the Kon-Tiki, a balsa log raft on which he traveled nearly 5000 miles from Peru to Polynesia. Experts predicted the Kon-Tiki would become water-logged and sink within days, but Heyerdahl pushed forward any-way, despite being deadly afraid of deep water.[1]

Heyerdahl overcame his fear of the water in a big way. Another person might have overcome this fear by taking a trip on a ship. Heyerdahl, however, navigated the oceans in a log raft. He learned to love the waves and the open ocean.

Heyerdahl did not let fear hold him prisoner. He let his hope and Kon-Tiki carry him to new discoveries and distant shores. Heyerdahl possessed what Napoleon Hill called a positive mental attitude. A person with that attitude has "plus" characteristics, such as faith, hope, and optimism.[2]

Don't let fear prevent you from pursuing your dreams and your passion, whatever they may be, because it's what life is all about. Erik R. Lindbergh dreamed of duplicating his grand-father's groundbreaking, nonstop, solo flight in 1927 across the Atlantic. His grandfather, Charles Lindbergh, flew the monowing *Spirit of St. Louis* from New York to Paris in 33½ hours, a trip that proved fatal for several other pilots who previously tried. Unfortunately, Erik Lindbergh was forced to put his dream on hold due to the crippling effects of arthritis.

But Erik Lindbergh did not give up. After taking a new drug that mitigated his arthritic problem, he was able to resume flying and recreated his grandfather's dangerous flight across the Atlantic. Flying in *The New Spirit of St. Louis*, Erik made the trip in 16 hours. He also recreated his grandfather's flights from San Diego to St. Louis, and from St. Louis to New York.[3]

Charles Lindbergh sometimes flew the *Spirit of St. Louis* less than 100 feet above the ocean. All he had to eat were a few sandwiches and two canteens of water. He did not have the sophisticated navigational and safety equipment that his grandson's plane carried. In fact, Lindbergh fashioned a crude periscope, so he could see beyond the fuel tank on the front of the plane.

Both Charles and Erik Lindbergh did not let fear stand in the way of their dream. Successful people find a way to live the life they've imagined, while others never run out of excuses. Many people claim that they're too busy with work or family to accomplish anything else. They blame their lack of success on the fact that they don't have time to do anything else but work.

The Stockdale Perspective on Faith and Hope

On September 9, 1965, James Stockdale, a Navy fighter pilot, was shot down by antiaircraft fire on a bombing mission over North Viet Nam. Stockdale broke his back when he ejected himself from the aircraft.[4]

He was captured as soon as his parachute dropped to earth and was held prisoner for nearly eight years in a North Vietnamese prison. He survived the horrendous experience by stoically accepting his fate and impassively enduring all of the cruel treatment he received at the hands of his captors. Stockdale was tortured over 20 times from 1965 through 1973. Even though it would mean more torture if discovered, Stockdale implemented an internal communication system, so fellow prisoners would feel less isolated. Despite the risk, Stockdale sent secret intelligence information to his wife in his letters.[5]

Stockdale made a resolution to be a symbol of resistance and deliberately wounded himself to show his captors he would rather die than surrender. At one point, Stockdale cut himself with a razor and beat himself with a stool, so he would not be videotaped.[6] Stockdale was later awarded the Congressional Medal of Honor. He became the first three-star officer in the history of the Navy to wear both aviator wings and the Congressional Medal of Honor. He was one of the most highly decorated officers in the history of his service, wearing 26 personal combat decorations including four Silver Stars.

An indomitable spirit is built on hope. You believe in certain principles and hope that in the end you'll triumph. But even though you're hopeful, you still must deal with the realities of your situation.

A Message from Garcia

Many people hope for success but fear failure. Fear can paralyze you into a life of tolerance and drudgery. Fear can prevent you from taking the steps that could lead to a new, different, better life. No great achievement has ever been attained without first confronting that fear, followed by a leap of faith and a heart filled with hope. Hope is the secret antidote to cure you of any fear you may have, the emotional counterbalance to tip the scale of success in your favor.

If you do not believe in your success, no one else will. If you do not clearly see your goal or dream, no one else can. You must repel all negative energy that can distract you from achieving your goals and replace it with unwavering faith in your ability to succeed against all odds. If hope can propel the peoples of a nation to rise against oppression and tyranny in pursuit of a better life, hope can inspire you to the greatest levels of individual achievement. Faith and hope occupy the two sides of the same coin used in the bank of emotions we draw on in our quest for success. Jingle your pocket regularly to remind you of your faith and the hope you hold in your heart for the success you seek.

CHAPTER 22

·······································

Rise and Shine, and Fall in Line

WHEN I WAS 24 YEARS OLD AND IN THE AIR FORCE, I SAW AN AD IN a magazine for the White House Fellows program. I knew immediately it was something I wanted to do. When I finally received the materials, I put them on my nightstand and every night before going to bed I read about the program, all the while thinking about how I might be able to become a White House Fellow. I was constantly thinking about the White House Fellows program and asking people whom I thought might know something about it for their opinion on the program.

One such occurrence took place during a meeting I had in Panama with Mort Zuckerman, the publisher of *U.S. News and World Report*, and General Galvin. Because I was so focused on the White House Fellows program, I made that goal part of my persona. During this meeting between Zuckerman and General Galvin, I mentioned my desire to become a White House Fellow. As it turned out, Zuckerman was a member of the White House Fellows regional selection panel in Boston, and he graciously volunteered to write me a letter of recommendation.

Zuckerman also said it would be helpful to have a recommendation from someone who knew my work, such as General Galvin. General Galvin not only wrote me a nice letter of recommendation, but he also told me to contact General Bernard Loeffke, the

141

commanding general of U.S. Army South in Panama, because he had been a White House Fellow in the early 1970s.

General Loeffke was an Army major general whom I had met when giving presentations to distinguished visitors concerning our military strategy in Latin America. I called General Loeffke's office to make an appointment. The aide said, "The general will see you tomorrow at 0500 hours, and bring your M-14."

"Oh," I replied, and paused. My mind was reeling. Quickly I said, "Well, the Air Force doesn't supply us with M-14s."

"No problem," said the aide, "the Army has plenty of extra M-14s, and we'll find one for you."

"Okay," I said. I was about to say goodbye when the aide added "And oh, by the way, you'll be joining the general on a two-mile run in full gear with backpack."

"Sure, that will be fine," I said, and hung up the phone. I was doomed. I could not believe what I just got myself into. In the Air Force we fly, we don't run on the ground. This is not what I expected. For those of you nonmilitary types, 0500 hours is 5:00 A.M and an M-14 is a rifle. The standard M-14 weighs about nine pounds, unloaded. I was not used to running early in the morning with a backpack and a rifle; this would be interesting.

Before I met the general, I did a little research to learn what I could about him. First, the general had a brilliant mind. A West Point graduate from the class of 1957, he had an undergraduate degree in engineering, a master's degree in Russian, and a doctorate in political science and spoke fluent Russian, Chinese, French, Spanish, and Portuguese. In 1970, he was an aide to Henry Kissinger, responsible for analyzing events in the Soviet Union, Vietnam, and Latin America. In the mid-1970s, he served as chief of the military mission in the People's Republic of China, and later served as the U.S. Army attaché in the former Soviet Union during the Brezhnev era.

Second, the general was tough as nails. In Vietnam, he served in the 82nd Airborne Division Special Forces and as an advisor to a Vietnamese parachute battalion, earning two Purple Hearts for wounds in combat and several Valor awards for heroism. An Airborne Ranger, he was the first Westerner to jump with a regular Chinese communist parachute unit. He later served as chief of staff of the 18th Airborne Corps at Fort Bragg, North Carolina.

Third, the General had a magnetic personality. In Vietnam, General Loeffke angered the headquarters' brass by rewarding the top-performing enlisted men in his unit by allowing one man each night to sleep in his tent, while he took their place on the front lines. Fourth, the General was a physical fitness nut. He was a champion swimmer at West Point, he competed in a military decathalon in Russia, and he ran a full-length marathon in Communist China. His fanaticism for physical fitness almost created an international incident. While in the former Soviet Union, his exercise regime included running in the morning in shiny combat boots and a rifle. One morning, the Moscow police detained him. When they finally sorted it all out, as the story goes, he continued his early morning runs with combat boots and a rifle; however, the negotiated settlement called for the Russian Army to provide him with a fake wooden rifle, of the exact weight of the one he ran with.

As if all this wasn't intimidating enough, I also learned that at the conclusion of the early morning runs with his troops, the general invited soldiers to engage him in hand-to-hand combat in what was called the "bear pit." The General would take his position in a mud pit surrounded by a wall of sand bags, and enlisted men were encouraged to enter and pummel him if possible. Most soldiers' visions of pummeling the General quickly vanished when they entered the pit; the General was a fierce fighting machine. To really motivate the soldiers, the General offered a three-day pass to any soldier who could throw him over the wall surrounding the bear pit.

Armed with this knowledge, I awoke early and met General Loeffke the next day at 5:00 A.M. It was still dark out as I made my way to the staging area where I would meet the general. The jungle was alive with the early morning sounds of a new day, birds and jungle critters each contributing their chorus to this morning symphony.

When I approached General Loeffke, I remember thinking that he was the poster image of an Army General. He was over six feet tall, with a shaved bald head that shimmered in the moonlight. He was slim and fit, with very broad shoulders and narrow hips, the body of an Olympic swimmer. "Good morning, sir," I said loudly as I approached. I am sure the animal varmints thought I was deaf. Soldiers don't just speak to each other; it's more like a yell. I assumed yelling would be good.

"At ease, soldier," he snapped back. My decision to yell was good; he was yelling too. "Lieutenant, fall in next to me," he ordered. In the two seconds he took to give me a command, I knew he was sizing me up. I promptly took a sharp turn and found a spot behind him but in front of the troops assembled for this morning's run.

Shortly after the run commenced, I found myself alongside the General. We ran this way for about a mile. He did not break a sweat and just seemed to glide along as his shiny combat boots hit the pavement like pistons. He was focused on the road. He never once looked at me; he never once spoke to me. I dared not say a word. It was a game of poker, and the first to flinch loses. I was not going to flinch. Inside I was dying. I was sure he was able to hear my heart ready to burst out of my chest. Then, at about the mile and a half mark, he turned his head and looked at me. "It wouldn't be quite right if an Army General crossed the finish line at the same time as an Air Force Lieutenant," he said.

The General turned his head away from me and threw his clutch into fifth gear. He was gone. If the enemy was behind me with bullets whizzing over my head I could not have run faster, or ever caught up to the General. I saw my White House Fellowship quickly vanishing over the horizon. During the balance of the run I was thinking of alternative careers. Civilian life isn't all that bad. I finished the run and went to work, in an emotional state somewhere between depression and exhaustion.

Later that day, I was at my desk and the phone rang. "Lieutenant Garcia," said the steely voice on the other end. "This is General Loeffke's aide."

"Yes," I said. I was surprised but tried not to reveal it in my voice.

"The General would like to see you tomorrow at 5 o'clock."

"Is that 0500 hours?" I responded, praying it wasn't.

"No, he will see you at 1700 hours."

Thank goodness, I thought to myself. 1700 hours is 5 P.M.

"Will we be running or will I need a weapon?" I asked with trepidation.

"No, you will be meeting the general in his office. Anything else, Lieutenant Garcia?" the aide snapped with a hint of annoyance.

"No, that will be all," I said. I hung up the phone and still had the image of the General disappearing over the hill in the jungle.

I met the General in his office the next day, sans fatigues, and the meeting went extremely well. The General was sympathetic to my cause and, much to my surprise, I felt that he took great pleasure in mentoring a young officer. In addition to being a White House Fellow in 1970, he told me that he was appointed in 1973 as the executive director of the program for one year, responsible for the education and travel schedule of the current class, as well as the recruitment of the new White House Fellows.

He enjoyed telling me that one of his recruits was a rising military man, Colin Powell. In 1973, Loeffke appointed Powell for his fellowship year to work for Frank Carlucci, who was then the Director of the Office of Management and Budget. Carlucci later became the Secretary of Defense and was very helpful. Of course, Powell went on to become the Chairman of the Joint Chiefs of Staff and in January 2001, was appointed as the Secretary of State under President George W. Bush.

Meanwhile, back at the General's office, General Loeffke was kind enough to spend an hour with me, pointing out the ins and outs of the application process, the pros and cons of the program, what to expect, what not to expect, and the best way to approach the interview process if I advanced to the regional or national panels. At the end of our meeting, instead of getting a beating in the sand pit, he offered to write me a letter of recommendation. With his help, I formulated a strategy to pursue my desire of becoming a White House Fellow. I was ultimately successful, and now serve on the Board of Directors of the White House Fellows Foundation.

Focus on Your Goals Every Day of the Year

Years ago, actor Jim Carrey vowed to become a movie star and sign a movie deal worth $12 million. To guarantee that he would stay focused on this goal, Carrey wrote a check to himself for $12 million. Obviously, he couldn't cash the check because it would have bounced higher than his face stretched in *The Mask*.

Carrey folded up that check and carried it around with him in his wallet. When he wrote it, Carrey had just given up his stand-up comedy career and had joined the cast of the television show "In Living Color." From that program, Carrey moved on to a hugely successful movie career. All the while, he carried with him the $12 million check that he had written to himself years earlier. Carrey's goal was to become a major motion picture star, and the uncashed check helped him visualize that goal. After several successful movies, Carrey hit the big time with his role as The Joker in *Batman Forever*. His payday for making that film was no joke. Carrey made $12 million.[1]

In 1970, actor Bruce Lee wrote himself a letter predicting that he would be the best-known Asian movie star in the United States by 1980 and would have earned $10 million by that time. Although Lee's life ended tragically as a young man, he did reach his goal before he died. Running back Ricky Williams set the goal of winning the Heisman Trophy. According to Associated Press reporter Richard Rosenblatt, Williams even created an e-mail address that included Heisman.com. In 1998, the University of Texas football player won the prestigious award.[2]

Dr. Kevin Elko, a performance consultant in McDonald, Pennsylvania, distinguishes between product goals and process goals. A product goal is what you are going to achieve. A process goal is a prescription for success, which is the plan you must follow to achieve your product goal. According to Dr. Elko, it is the process that gets us to our ultimate aspiration. To reach the destination, we must see the reward. Whether it's writing a check to yourself or writing down your objectives on a piece of paper, the act of visualizing the product goal helps turn the dream into a reality.

A Message from Garcia

Once you know what it is you want to do, you must be crystal clear about that goal and focus on it constantly. Write it down. Paste it on your mirror. Stick it on your dashboard. Keep it in your wallet. Focus on that goal daily and record it into your subconscious mind. By doing so, during the course of your daily activities, when certain situations or circumstances occur, your subconscious mind will move you toward the achievement of that goal. Maybe you'll say something to someone you might not normally speak to. This could trigger an encounter or a reaction that might result in moving you closer to achieving your goal. You will be amazed at the power of activating the potential energy that is stored in your being and the power that it has to attract all the things that are necessary to achieve your dreams.

CHAPTER 23

Embrace Diversity

WHEN IT COMES TO CELEBRATING OUR DIVERSITY, I CAN THINK OF no better example than Dr. Martin Luther King Jr. Despite the imagery he painted in his most famous speech while standing on the steps of the Lincoln Memorial before a crowd of 300,000 in 1963, saying, "I have a dream," Martin Luther King was no idle dreamer. In addition to being one of this nation's greatest leaders, he also possessed the attributes of a successful entrepreneur. He had a revolutionary idea. He was an apostle of action. He was a man who would not quit, and ultimately, he died pursuing his dream. Above all else, he taught us that "the ultimate measure of an individual is not where they stand in moments of comfort, but where they stand in times of challenge and controversy."

At the age of 15, Martin Luther King Jr. entered Morehouse College in Atlanta, Georgia, under a special program for gifted students, receiving his bachelor of arts degree in sociology in 1948. As an undergraduate, his earlier interests in medicine and law were replaced by a desire to enter the ministry. Spending the next three years at Crozer Theological Seminary in Chester, Pennsylvania, he studied Mohandas Gandhi's philosophy of nonviolence. Through Gandhi's emphasis on love and nonviolence he discovered the method of social reform that he had been seeking. He also studied the philosophy of contemporary Protestant theologians and was recognized as the most outstanding student in his class, receiving the J. Lewis Crozer Fellowship for graduate study at a university of his choice. He was also elected president of the student body and delivered the valedictory address, earning a bachelor's degree in divinity in 1951.

From Crozer he went to Boston University, where he studied the history of philosophy, and examined in depth the philosophy of Plato, Hegel, and Alfred North Whitehead, and the works of Reinhold Niebuhr. He earned a Ph.D. in systematic theology in 1955. Despite a schedule that included his family, his church, the Southern Christian Leadership Conference, his world travels, and his many speaking engagements, Dr. King managed to write six books. I learned many valuable lessons from his writings that I have applied in my own life, and I highly recommend the following books that he wrote:

- *Stride Toward Freedom: The Montgomery Story* (New York, Harper & Row, 1958). Dr. King's first book; the story of the Montgomery bus boycott and start of the nonviolent civil rights movement.
- *The Measure of a Man* (Philadelphia, Pilgrim Press, 1959). A selection of Dr. King's sermons.
- *Why We Can't Wait* (New York: Harper & Row, 1963). Edited by James M. Washington. The story of the Birmingham campaign and the essential writings of Dr. King.
- *Strength to Love* (New York, Harper & Row, 1963). A selection of Dr. King's most requested sermons.
- *Where Do We Go From Here: Chaos or Community?* (New York, Harper & Row, 1967). Reflections on the problems of his day and America's priorities.
- *The Trumpet of Conscience* (New York, Harper & Row, 1968). The 1967 Massey Lectures sponsored by the Canadian Broadcasting Corporation (posthumously). Dr. King addresses issues including the Vietnam war, youth, and civil disobedience and concludes with the "Christmas Sermon for Peace."

King took the theological philosophy and the insights gained from his academic training and transformed these ideas into concrete actions, forcing our nation's leaders to examine their own conscience. He used his political genius, his intellect, and his persuasive power to make civil rights a moral issue that could no longer be ignored.

You might wonder why, as a Hispanic American, I would focus on Martin Luther King. The reason is simple. It is because Martin Luther King fought for and earned rights that have benefited not just African-Americans, but all of us. We can honor him every day by taking personal accountability for excellence in everything we do, and being tenacious when it comes to making our dreams a reality.

Success in the Face of Discrimination

When Benjamin O. Davis Jr. died in July 2002, we lost much more than another four-star general. We lost a brave African-American man who had fought wars both on and off the battlefield. This Air Force general, whose combat record was exemplary, played a major role in triggering the integration of the armed forces after World War II.[1]

During World War II, racial segregation plagued the United States military. Black aviators were trained at a military base in the town of Tuskegee, Alabama. The aviators trained at that base became known as the Tuskegee Airmen.

General Davis, a colonel at the time, was the commanding officer of these men in the war in Europe against Germany. He and his pilots escorted bombers on 200 European combat missions during World War II. Not one of the bombers protected by his men was lost due to Nazi attacks. The all-black unit's heroism in World War II is well documented and paved the way for integration of the armed forces.

Men like Davis and the Tuskegee Airmen faced battles in the air, as well as fights on the home front so that they could be treated as equals. The Air Force I served in welcomed men and women from all walks of life. Nevertheless, there are diversity issues in almost every organization.

Adjusting to a Different Culture Isn't Easy

On my first day at the Air Force Academy, I struck up a conversation with one of my new classmates. During our chat, he made a joke that used a phrase I had never heard before and laughed quite loudly at his own story. He must have noticed the blank look on my face and explained that the expression was from *Mork and Mindy*, a television show that I had never heard of.

My classmate explained that the program was about a space alien, played by Robin Williams, who comes to earth. Williams' character, Mork, is unfamiliar with the customs, habits, traditions, and language of humans, and his inappropriate behavior is what generates the laughs. More than once during my first days among my peers at the Academy, I felt like Mork.

Although I did not feel discriminated against at the Academy, I did feel odd at times. I had a more pronounced accent at the time, and although I've lost the accent, there's something in the intonation of my voice, even today, that makes it sound as if I'm asking a question, rather than making a statement. Gradually, I was able to adjust to life in the United States. My parents taught me English when I was growing up in Panama, so my understanding of the language tremendously facilitated my ability to adapt to these new customs, including television shows. What also helped were the summers with my grandfather in Daytona Beach, and the long conversations we had in English.

For many immigrants, the adjustment to life in America is much more dramatic and difficult, sometimes paralyzing, and always overwhelming. They struggle to learn the language, and they likely always will speak with an accent that often is difficult to understand. Even more challenging than learning the words themselves is grasping the concepts behind the grammar and pop culture references like those portrayed on *Mork and Mindy*. If you've lived somewhere else all your life, imagine trying to understand a figure of speech such as "You take the cake." If you haven't spoken English all your life, how hard is it to understand why "fat chance" and "slim chance" mean the same thing? How about trying to make sense out of "it's raining cats and dogs?"

By my senior year at the academy, I felt that I belonged. I led my squadron in parade formation as we entered a football stadium for an important game against our most fierce rival, Notre Dame. As we marched on to the field, a falcon, the Air Force mascot, flew across the cloudless blue sky. The stands were packed with thousands of cheering football fans. I carried a saber that was extended directly in front of me, and the sunlight reflected off its gleaming blade. As we marched onto the field, my name was announced over the loudspeaker: "Charles Garcia, Deputy Wing Commander, from the Republic of Panama."

At that moment, I felt I could never accomplish anything greater than leading my squadron onto the field in front of a stadium full of people. On that day, I felt my dreams had come true.

A Message from Garcia

Respect for diversity is a characteristic of successful people. They avoid generalizations and look beyond an individual's ethnicity. The successful entrepreneur appreciates having employees with diverse backgrounds and knows it can improve the company's bottom line. Diversity initiatives have been shown to have a positive effect on morale and productivity. Those initiatives can also lead to improved customer service and market penetration.

Too many people improperly generalize about minorities, relying on stereotypes to form predisposed judgments about a person or class of people. Oddly, this includes members of minority groups who themselves frequently have biases about members of their own ethnic group, as well as others. Hispanics, for example, are not a homogenous group. Hispanics comprise a number of separate and distinct races and cultures that share language as a common thread. Among these groups there are subtle differences between the various Spanish-speaking countries. Most Americans fail to recognize these distinctions and many members of the Hispanic community at large subscribe to their own biases as well.

Successful people look at the individual, not at where they are from and how they speak. The key measure should always be their individual skills, capabilities, and talents. Successful people view people in terms of their contribution *because* of these differences, i.e., race, culture, religion, and age, and not despite them. Prejudice, just like fear, can prevent an individual from achieving their dreams in life.

CHAPTER 24

....

Age Is Not a Barrier
to Success

YOU'RE NEVER TOO OLD TO HAVE GOALS OR THE DESIRE TO PURSUE your dreams. As you age, you might not be able to win golf's grand slam, but your goals can be every bit as meaningful to you. In *Passages,* Gail Sheehy spoke of three "adulthoods." The third adulthood begins at about age 60. In the third adulthood, you discover who you are and begin to take back your life. Essentially, you restart your life. Perhaps you take up a new hobby or volunteer your time for a good cause. It's a good time to pursue your passion, if you haven't already. If you haven't found your passion yet, think about what you loved to do as a child and go from there. In that third adulthood, you should repair a bad relationship or let it go.

Take the case of the 61-year-old woman at Barry University in Miami, Florida, who is doing more than just going to school. She also played on the golf team and helped lead Barry University to a second-place finish at the NCAA Division II South Region Women's Golf Championship.[1]

The name Judy Eller may be familiar to you, since she won the U.S. Junior Golf Championship in 1957 and 1958 while a student at the University of Miami. In 1959 she was the NCAA champion. A year later she played on the American team that won the Curtis Cup.

In 1961, Eller married Gordon Street and quit playing golf to raise her four children. Her return to golf, like her return to college, was accidental, when she attended a Barry University athletic awards dinner, and met the golf coach Roger White. Although it began as a joke, the fact was that Eller Street still had some four semesters of eligibility left for Division II play.

In 2001, Eller Street enrolled as a student, got in shape, lost 20 pounds, and hit the links. During a typical school day, she competes with golfers a third her age, carrying her bag for 36 holes, before driving 25 miles back to the university campus to take an exam.[2] The good news is that after the first 8 tournament rounds she sported an 84.6 stroke average.

Age did not hold back Helen Hooven Santmyer, either. Her first book, *And Ladies of the Club*, was a best seller with over 2 million books in print. She was in her eighties when the book came out. Another writer, Mildred Benson, was still at her desk at the *Toledo Blade* at age 96. Benson was the oldest working journalist in the country when she died in May 2002. Not only did Benson pursue her dream of being a journalist, she inspired millions of girls to pursue their dreams. Benson was the author of the first 23 Nancy Drew mysteries. Written under the pseudonym Carolyn Keene, Benson's books showed girls they could be smart and adventurous.[3] Benson herself was adventurous and daring. At age 59, she took up flying and earned her commercial and private pilot licenses. She took a canoe trip through the jungles of Central America with only natives to guide her.

Put on a New Set of Tires and Get Rolling

Stanley H. Kaplan, founder of the Kaplan Educational Centers, is still out on the stump giving speeches, and he wrote a book at age 82. In response to a reporter's question, Kaplan said that he was not retiring, just putting on new tires.

There are many other examples of older people in hot pursuit of their dreams. At age 70, Louisiana governor Mike Foster was enrolled in law school. An 80-year-old retired government employee received his Ph.D. in urban studies. Colonel Sanders was no spring chicken when he finally hit success in the chicken business; the Colonel was in his 60s when KFC finally took off. Grandma Moses was well up in years when her painting career also took off. Colonel Tom Parker wasn't getting any younger when he discovered Elvis Presley.[4]

Former senator John Glenn dreamed of returning to space. He first orbited the earth three times in Friendship 7 in 1962. In 1998, at the age of 77, he was aboard the space shuttle *Discovery*. Glenn overcame his age and jokes that the space shuttle traveled in the left lane with its turn signal on, a reference to the stereotypical older driver.

From Hero to Healer

Bernard "Burn" Loeffke, with whom I had that most memorable 5:00 A.M. full pack and rifle run, has since retired from the military after a nearly 40-year career and has gone on to continue his extraordinary achievements. At the age of 62, Burn is pursuing his original dream, despite being sidetracked by an exemplary military career.

As a youngster, Loeffke had always dreamed of being a doctor as he traveled the world with his parents. His father was a college professor and his mother a well-to-do Spaniard who instilled in him a great love of language and culture. They lived in Paris, South America, and finally upstate New York, where he was a champion swimmer. When he was recruited to West Point for his swimming prowess, the dream of a life in medicine dissipated.[5]

When he retired, Loeffke was offered top private-sector jobs selling weapons and cars in China. But there was never any doubt about what he would do when his military service was complete—medical missions for the impoverished. To achieve this dream, Loeffke spent two years attending a program to become a physician's assistant, a medical degree that allows him to perform about two-thirds of the procedures that fully licensed MDs do. He decided not to pursue an MD because it would take too long. He graduated from the physician assistant program at Nova Southeastern University in Davie in 1997.

Despite retiring, the General does not appear to be slowing down, in fact, quite the contrary. Since 1997 his work as a medical missionary has taken him to Afghanistan, Cambodia, China, Guatemala, Guyana, Sudan, and Vietnam. He also studies and teaches leadership courses, and studies and writes about philosophy. He is almost obsessive about staying physically fit, running five miles every day along Hollywood beach. Nine years from now, when he is 75, he hopes to complete Hawaii's Ironman competition—a two-mile ocean swim, 150 miles on a bike, and then a 26-mile running marathon.[6]

A Message from Garcia

Success is achievable at any age. Of course, when you're younger it's easier and more realistic to aspire toward certain dreams that are not achievable as you age, particularly those that are based on physical achievement.

Even as we age it is healthy to continue to work toward improving ourselves as human beings, which includes keeping your mind as active as possible as well as engaging in some type of physical activity. Whether it's mastering a new computer program, learning to knit, or playing backgammon, bridge, or shuffleboard—activities that are less demanding physically—you can always expose yourself to new experiences, increase your knowledge, and participate in activities that sustain your health. Volunteering to work for charitable causes and working on important projects in the community can also keep you vital and young at heart. As you age, it's important to remain as active as possible by exercising your mind as well as your body. Successful people of any age should look to the future rather than dwell on the past. Keep your mind filled with dreams and goals.

PART FOUR

SUCCESS STRATEGY 2: START PLANNING NOW

CHAPTER 25

························

Preparation Is Everything . . . and Then Some

RAY AND ROSE CHAVEZ KNOW THE VALUE OF PREPARATION. Although Mr. and Mrs. Chavez never went beyond high school, they wanted their kids to go college—and all five of their children graduated from college.

Starting when the children were young, the parents limited the amount of time they could watch television. They also read to them until they were old enough to read themselves. To prepare their children for school and life, the Chavezes made sacrifices. Any extra money was used to buy books and encyclopedias instead of vacations and big cars.

The hard work, dedication, and commitment of Ray and Rose Chavez have paid enormous dividends. In 2001, Elena, the youngest, graduated from Harvard with honors. Elena, however, was not the first Chavez to go to college and graduate. She was the fifth Chavez sibling to graduate from Harvard. Thanks to the sacrifices of their parents, all five children received a first-rate education and are thoroughly prepared to make their mark in the world.[1]

There are books about every imaginable career. Find them, and read them. They will give you great insights into whatever it is you may want pursue in your life. In fact, it's a great thing to do while you are searching for a mentor. It might even help you find one. At the least, you'll demonstrate that you have done your homework, that you are familiar, to some extent, with the career field that you have chosen, and that will invariably convince your prospective mentor, or even potential employer, about the intensity of your interest, pushing you head and shoulders above other candidates.

Your reading shouldn't be limited to work-related books. A committee of New York educators and cultural leaders went on a mission to find books that would encourage more young people and adults to read. *The Color of Water* was chosen as the first book New Yorkers should read.[2]

It's no wonder *The Color of Water* was selected. This book by James C. McBride tells the true story of what it was like to grow up in Harlem, Brooklyn, and Queens with 11 siblings. McBride's father was an African-American Baptist minister and his mother was a Yiddish-speaking Polish immigrant whose father was a rabbi.

McBride's mother, Rachel, was a strong-willed woman who believed strongly in religion and education. When she married a black man, her relatives sat *shiva* for her, the Hebrew prayer that is said when someone dies. She converted to Christianity and helped her husband build a Baptist church in Brooklyn.

After her husband died, Rachel married another African-American man. He raised her eight children and they had four more children together. They were extremely poor and their living conditions were difficult. The boys were packed in one room and the girls in another.[3] Through it all, McBride's mother preached the value of education, saying that money doesn't mean anything if your mind is empty.

Rachel's children took her words to heart. All 12 children went on to college and most earned advanced degrees. McBride holds a master's degree in journalism from Columbia University and is an accomplished saxophone player and composer. At age 65, his mother Rachel earned a degree in social work from Temple University. McBride once asked his mother if God were black or white. *The Roanoke Times & World News* reported that she replied, "God is the color of water. Water does not have a color."

A Message from Garcia

Planning and preparation are essential ingredients to success. If you have a passion for a particular career or industry, you'll want to learn everything you can about it. During the course of this self-education you might be able to find a mentor. You probably won't get Bill Gates or Warren Buffett as a mentor, but reading about their philosophy and strategies is surely the next best thing.

I first read about Buzzy Schwartz, one of Wall Street's legendary traders, in *Market Wizards*, a book about the financial giants on Wall Street. This inspired me to seek him out as a mentor. I never would have known about him if I hadn't read this book, and my career might have gone off in a different direction. After I read about the White House Fellows program, I focused on being selected as a White House Fellow. Unquestionably, if I had not been selected to join the White House Fellows program, my life also would have taken a different path. Finding a good mentor in life is often the tipping point towards the realization of your dreams. Work hard to find someone that can help you in the area that you have chosen to pursue.

CHAPTER 26

Successful People Are Creative

ENTREPRENEURS CAN ENHANCE THEIR CREATIVITY BY PIGGYBACKING on the ideas of others. Robert Hargrove distinguished between two types of entrepreneurs—those who create something new or practice creative imitation. With creative imitation, entrepreneurs identify profitable opportunities in a field where they already have expertise, and creatively imitate by building on another company's idea and taking a different approach.[1] Even Sam Walton, the founder of Wal-Mart, said that some of his best ideas came from watching how others ran their business.

Arthur K. Melin cofounded the company that popularized the Frisbee in the 1950s. But Edward E. Headrick took this great idea and made it even better. Headrick added the grooves to the Frisbee and cut down on the drag. The concentric grooved ridges or "spoilers" that Headrick added cut down on the aerodynamic resistance. The end result was that a novice Frisbee player could throw farther and with more accuracy.[2]

The National Federation of Independent Businesses conducted a survey of small business owners to find out how they spend their day. The survey found that 42 percent of business owners' time is spent in operations. Sales and marketing take up 22 percent of their time. Only 10 percent of the time is spent on planning and strategy. It appears that small business owners aren't thinking creatively about ways to make their business grow.

Be Still and Breed Brilliance

When was the last time you had a great idea? Can you imagine having to come up with great ideas all the time? Some businesses, like advertising, require just that. Advertising is the idea business. Some people are more creative than others but everybody can develop skills that allow exploring and developing creativity.

Paula Ancona offers advice on nurturing creativity. She suggests keeping an "idea list." Ancona also suggests that you broaden your horizons. Take up new hobbies, or try something that might be out of character for you. Vary your routine by taking a different route to work or having lunch with a different group of people.[3] Build unstructured thinking time into your schedule.

I find that meditating is a great way to come up with ideas. The concept of clearing your mind while at the same time focusing on a specific solution might sound contradictory. Yet when you are quiet, peaceful, and you "open your mind" to the energy of the universe, you will come upon many great ideas and solutions to the issues that you meditate on.

Napoleon Hill recommended that on a daily basis you engage in studying, thinking, and planning how to achieve your goals. Hill suggested that you write down precisely and concisely your plan of action. The written statement should say exactly what you want and exactly when you want it. Hill contended, "Whatever your mind can conceive, you can achieve."[4]

Brian Tracy advocates the practice of solitude and contemplation and writes, "If ever you desire an answer to any question, a solution to any dilemma, or the resolution to any difficulty, practice solitude. Go and sit quietly by yourself, with no noise or distraction, for 60 minutes. It has been said that men and women begin to become great when they begin to spend time alone with themselves, listening to their inner voices." "At a certain moment," Tracy writes, "ideas and insights will flow through your mind."[5]

Distractions are everywhere. From the moment we open our eyes in the morning to the moment we shut them before we go to bed, something is competing for our attention. We doze off to sleep to the humming sound of television or music, that last commercial still buzzing in our ears. Or we might read until words get blurry and our eyelids beg for mercy. Every morning, like about 120 million other Americans, we probably start the day with that same radio station, or by turning on the TV.

Television is probably the single biggest distraction in our lives. Television is the antithesis of thinking. It does the thinking for you. Is it possible to get ideas from watching television? Absolutely. But how do you expect to develop these brilliant ideas if you keep numbing your brain with a constant flow of bright pictures and loud noise?

I challenge you right now. Take a problem you're now facing or consider the single most important thing on your mind right now. Take that problem, keep it in your mind, and go sit somewhere. Find a quiet space, inside or outside of your home. Then just close your eyes and try to clear your mind. Do not think of anything in particular, or maybe just think about silence and try to clear your mind like a blank blackboard. What will happen is that after 10 or 15 minutes you will get flashes of ideas into your head. They will be all sorts of extraneous thoughts. Things that you didn't even know you were thinking about will surface.

When you really learn to meditate, you can control your thinking, and what you will find is that your mind is actually a magnet for ideas. Things will simply just come to you. The point is that quiet, solitude, and simple thinking time are *essential* for the creation of new ideas.

A Message from Garcia

Creativity breeds success. By being creative you will continually work on developing new and innovative ways to solve problems. This means that you need to make time to think. Find a quiet spot and clear your mind of all distractions. Ideas are the springboard to improved performance at work and to the planning or growth of your business. Give yourself the opportunity to think and generate new ideas.

In addition, you can build upon the ideas of others. Brainstorming is a very dynamic process, and allows you to feed off the ideas of a group. When you brainstorm with others, you combine your creative energy. As a collaborative team you are more likely to arrive at a better idea than by yourself.

Remember to sleep with a notepad and pen by your bed. Some of my best ideas come in the middle of the night—when my mind is completely relaxed and works as a receptor of the energies of the universe.

CHAPTER 27

The Culture of Success

I FOUNDED STERLING FINANCIAL GROUP OF COMPANIES IN 1997. One of the principles I chose to immediately instill at the heart of Sterling was the culture of success. I learned this concept from John C. Whitehead, one of my mentors who was the cochairman of Goldman Sachs, one of the largest and arguably one of the most successful investment banks on Wall Street. I first met Whitehead when he hired me to work for him as a White House Fellow when he served as Deputy Secretary of State in the Reagan Administration. Much of our success came from following the Goldman Sachs model. It was easier to implement because I believed in it and there was no entrenched culture at my firm that had to be changed or eliminated. Here are some of the Goldman Sachs principles[1]:

- Our client's interests come before ours. If we serve those interests, we'll succeed.
- People, capital, and reputation are our most important assets.
- Teamwork is paramount. An individual can't put his or her personal interests ahead of the firm's or its clients'.
- Profits enhance our success because they replenish our capital and make this a firm where people want to work.
- We share those profits with the people who helped to create them.

Whitehead and Goldman Sachs believed the essence of the firm's existence was to serve the client. Everyone in the firm, from partners on down, owes a responsibility to the client.[2] Another key ingredient of Goldman Sach's success was to focus on the long term. By focusing on business five years from now, Goldman Sachs minimized the short-term greed that led to the demise of many Wall Street firms. Because of its commitment to meeting long-term goals, Goldman Sachs could continue to emphasize teamwork, low staff turnover, and customer service.[3] Having this culture of success has contributed greatly to our achievements, which have been numerous and include being named the fastest-growing Hispanic company in the United States by *Hispanic Business.*[4]

At Sterling, we don't make people wait for bonuses. When someone performs well, there is an immediate incentive award in his or her next paycheck. It's not necessarily the amount of money itself that counts the most, but the fact that this employee will realize that his or her good work doesn't go unnoticed.

Recognize a Job Well Done

To sustain a culture of success, employee retention is key. At my firm, we take pride in having little staff turnover, which is likely due in part to this type of recognition. Supervisors and managers should acknowledge people for good work and a job well done. This should be an everyday thing, and not just a once-in-a-while thing. If someone does good work, tell him or her so. Not only will your team like it, but everyone will work harder, maintain a good attitude, and continue to work with an enthusiastic spirit.

Acknowledgment means a great deal. Watch how people walk around your office. Do they walk briskly, or do they shuffle? Watch your employees' body language; it will tell you volumes about morale and attitude.

The reverse is also true. When people work hard for you and are aware that they're doing good work and are not being acknowledged, they often become bitter. This bitterness can rapidly stew into contempt and result in poor attitude, bad morale, and negative productivity. The following two sentences are incredibly simple but also very powerful. "Hey, good job, thanks for your hard work. I appreciate the time you put into that project; it really made a difference." These two sentences, spoken regularly when a job is in fact done well and the employee really has gone the extra mile, acknowledges that person for that hard work and will yield above-average results. It's called breeding a culture of success: when everyone feels good about their job, they work harder and do better. It's an extraordinary force multiplier. Imagine if every single employee on your staff worked 5 or even 10 percent harder, how much more profitable your company would be.

Positive reinforcement, motivational management, and pats on the back are second nature to good leaders and successful people. Great leaders, by definition, find unique ways to exemplify this principle. General Patton installed a radio system on a base and used it to recognize the efforts of his troops. He would say, "Found a good soldier today," and proceed to mention the man's name.[5]

I learned another effective tactic from General Galvin. He believed in writing notes congratulating a person for a job well done. Throughout my career, I noticed many of the exceptional people I worked with also wrote to their staff or colleagues. In fact, many of our presidents believed in writing personal notes as a way of expressing their gratitude. A note from the president is very powerful. Obviously, you don't have to be the president of the United States to write a letter that expresses gratitude. All people appreciate that, regardless from whom it comes.

The opposite behavior, according to management guru Ken Blanchard, is that which is carried out by a "seagull." He describes a seagull as a self-serving leader who likes to dump on people. The seagull flies in when you're doing something wrong. Leaders who are seagulls hate to hear negative feedback, because it makes them feel less omnipotent.[6] According to Blanchard, seagull managers have low self-esteem and are reluctant to share credit or power. They rarely praise the people who work for them. People rarely hear praise at work, mostly criticism. Too often, the only way that employees know if they're doing a good job is if they aren't getting chewed out.

You Can Create a Culture of Success at Home

You can even create a culture of success in your own home. Ask yourself what kind of messages you're sending to your children. Hopefully, you don't bring negative messages (or office supplies) home, which would influence how your children feel about work and success. Are you encouraging them to be a Lieutenant Rowan, the heroic figure in *A Message to Garcia* or are you sending less-than-positive messages?

Assuming your family sits down together at the dinner table, which is very important, ask yourself what messages you're conveying to your kids. Are you conveying the message that hard work doesn't get you anywhere and getting ahead is all about office politics, or are you teaching them positive lessons about being a success? Are you demonstrating the importance of integrity and honor by word and deed? Are you sending messages that encourage tolerance?

Even if your own workplace is less than ideal, don't sour your children on the importance of hard work. Maybe you're not getting the recognition you deserve at work, but your children should be recognized for their accomplishments. They should learn the value of teamwork, of seeing each family member working together toward a common goal.

As you pursue your passions, encourage your children to feel passionate about whatever excites them. Even if they pursue activities that you don't necessarily approve of, don't stand in their way. My father wasn't thrilled with my decision to apply to the Air Force Academy and pursue a military career, but he let me choose the path I wanted to follow. All of us must pursue our passions, not those of our parents. Of course, that doesn't mean parents must subsidize their children's pursuit of their passions.

As you develop a culture of success in your home, look at the impact of personality on personal achievement. Napoleon Hill has said that your personality is either your greatest asset or your greatest liability. Your personality shapes your thoughts, accomplishments, and relationships with others. According to Hill, a pleasing personality is a product of a positive mental attitude, tolerance, courtesy, sincerity, a sense of humor, patience, and other factors.[7] All of these factors can be a part of your family culture.

Andrea Jung, CEO of Avon, received inspiring advice from her mother. Jung wrote that her mother said, "Girls can do absolutely anything that boys can do. A woman can reach any height in any discipline if she works hard enough."[8]

A Message from Garcia

Just as you work hard to strive for excellence in delivering a quality product or service to your customers, you must also work hard to set high standards, ethics and a culture of success at your organization. While every member of the firm must take responsibility for adhering to a strong moral code, the example must clearly be set at the top. It is only then that the moral fiber of the firm will weave its way into every member of the organization, each of whom will then understand and employ these concepts in a positive attitude and with an exemplary work ethic. People enjoy knowing they work for a firm with a good reputation and will work hard to protect and preserve it.

A positive attitude is a catalyst for enhanced performance and both can be facilitated by acknowledgement and messages of positive reinforcement for a job well done, at all levels of the company's organizational chart. At every level of the corporate ladder, compliments and recognition for good performance should work its way down the ladder. This can be achieved through bonuses, large and small, a phone call acknowledging some achievement, both by email and by good old-fashioned handwritten notes.

Just as important, if not more so, is the need to create a culture of success in your own home. If you are single, then being a good and respectful son or daughter, and a good person to your brothers and sisters, will bring great joy to them and make your family proud. If you have a spouse, then being faithful and considerate of each other, and treating your relationship as a team with a sacred trust will allow you to accomplish the most challenging goals in your life. Not only are you your children's role model, but, put another way, you are their manager, their boss. If your boss acts a certain way and wants you to emulate that behavior, you pretty much have to do it—or else look for another job. Your children are in a similar position. You may want to fire them from time to time, but you're both pretty much stuck with each other. Set the standard and watch them follow. Instill in them a sense of pride and passion for whatever it is they do. Show them the way, but ultimately let them choose their own path (they will anyway). Just be sure you give them the tools to succeed when they reach that critical stage. The greatest gift you can give them is a moral compass, one built on integrity and honor. Do it and I guarantee that they will make you proud.

....

CHAPTER 28

Bring People In and Convince Them of Your Dream

SUCCESSFUL PEOPLE HAVE THE CAPACITY TO HOOK UP WITH THE most talented people to help them achieve their dream. Successful people are able to do this because they are passionate about whatever their dream is, and convey that dream with power and contagious enthusiasm. Entrepreneurs and leaders are visionaries. They paint the big picture, they can see their dream as though it were reality, and they can articulate it to others so they also see it. Most importantly, they convince others to become part of their dream, so much so that people might leave jobs where they have tenure, steady salaries, and profit sharing. Many people who join entrepreneurial endeavors uproot their families and relocate because they too believe in the dream and want to be part of it.

To succeed, of course, all these various talented players must be working in unison toward the same goal. In rural Reagan County, Texas, a 35-year-old high school science teacher and coach, Jim Morris, made a bet with the players on his terrible baseball team. In an inspirational moment, he gave his team a locker room speech and told them that if they won the district championship, he would try out for a major league baseball team. In his twenties, Morris had given up on baseball because of arm troubles and family responsibilities. With a renewed spirit and a common goal to rally around, the team bought into Morris's dream and went on to lead the standings in their district.

The high school science teacher kept his end of the bargain. Morris tried out for the Tampa Bay Devil Rays and was signed to a minor league contract. He made the majors and pitched two seasons as a reliever for the Devil Rays. Morris told his inspirational story in the book *The Oldest Rookie: Big League Dreams From A Small-Town Guy*[1], which later became a hit movie called *The Rookie*. In a tremendous twist, the producer of the movie actually played minor league baseball with Morris when both were starting out.

Whether you're the leader of a small town baseball team or a great leader like President Ronald Reagan, you need to bring people in and convince them of your dream. At the commencement address at the U.S. Air Force Academy in 1984, Ronald Reagan spoke these inspiring words: "But the greatest of all resources is the human mind; all other resources are discovered only through creative human intelligence. God has given us the ability to make something from nothing. And in a vibrant, open political economy, the human mind is free to dream, create, and perfect."

Share Your Dreams With Others

Jaime Escalante showed his students how to dream. He took underachieving students at Garfield High School in Los Angeles and inspired them with the dream of passing the advanced placement calculus exam. Those students bought into the dream and passed the exam in spite of the many barriers to their goal.

Sam Walton, founder of Wal-Mart, swayed others with his passion. Long before Wal-Mart was a household name, Walton lured talented executives to Arkansas by convincing them of his dream. His passion brought them from the cosmopolitan cities they lived in all the way to Arkansas and kept them there. They shared his dream, even though life at Wal-Mart was not what most executives expected. On many business trips, for example, they were required to share hotel rooms. Nevertheless, they bought into Walton's no-frills operation.

Walton made working at Wal-Mart fun and profitable for executives, as well as for employees at the other end of the salary spectrum. Wal-Mart was one of the first large companies to offer profit sharing to all levels of employees. In 1983, Walton promised that he would do a hula dance down Wall Street if Wal-Mart's profits reached a certain level. He kept that promise.[2]

Through their vision, passion, and energy leaders must create momentum for their employees and for the company to achieve its goals. Author John Maxwell postulates that true leaders motivate people, and it's this momentum that helps overcome every obstacle. Maxwell put a different slant on Harry Truman's famous line and said, "If you can't *make* some heat, get out of the kitchen."[3]

A Message from Garcia
....

Leaders are visionaries. Leaders convey the excitement for their venture with an energy and enthusiasm that is contagious, enabling them to convince others to buy into their dream, whatever it may be. While all parties on a journey toward the achievement of a dream set out on a voyage on uncertain seas, people are willing to board a ship whose captain they know is steering them toward an island of success.

Regardless of the inevitable stormy seas to be encountered on any business journey, the clouds will clear eventually and the swells will subside, so long as the captain is vigilant in his stewardship and never loses sight of the final destination and at all times remains passionate, courageous and invigorated with enthusiasm about the ultimate success of the enterprising voyage.

CHAPTER 29

··

Get the Right People
on the Bus

THROUGHOUT MY LIFE, I HAVE BEEN FORTUNATE TO BE SURROUNDED by great people. My father told me that if I wanted to create a great company, I'd have to surround myself with people who are a lot smarter than I am and let them do their jobs. He also taught me not to let my ego get in the way of running my business. Ronald Reagan gave similar advice. President Reagan said, "Surround yourself with the best people you can find, delegate authority and don't interfere."[1] James Stockdale offered an insightful observation about the power of leaders. He said, "Great leaders gain authority by giving it away."[2]

In February 1999, I hired Wall Street veteran Alexis Korybut as president of Sterling Financial. Korybut was a star institutional bond salesman for Solomon Smith Barney who had generated over $5 million a year in revenue and possessed an impressive list of Latin American clients.

Another of my original shareholders was John Curry, a former Notre Dame football player. He was accepted at the University of Buffalo Medical School, but spent the summer trading at the Chicago Board of Trade. Curry made $26,000 that summer, more than his father earned in one year. Instead of going on to medical school, Curry chose to pursue a career as a trader. Money was pouring in, yet Curry didn't do too well with his newly acquired wealth. After some tough times, Curry ended up working as a telemarketer, making cold calls to solicit contributions for the Hillsboro County, Florida fire fighters.

When he contacted me, interested in getting back in the trading business, and told me his story, I sensed he was a winner. I also knew that Sterling Financial could use his expertise in the fixed-income side of the business. John Curry has contributed enormously to the success of our firm and he subsequently became my first equity partner. In 2002, he executed over $60 billion worth of securities, and he personally makes more money in two weeks than I make in a year. He deserves every penny of it.

Sterling has come a long way since our humble beginnings. There were only three of us when we started, working out of what was once a broom closet at Bear Stearns, the financial services behemoth. Eventually, we were able to get more space, but we were in tight quarters for several years. Have you seen the commercials for an office supplies store that show the employees sharing one pen and writing notes on their body parts to save paper? Our situation wasn't quite that bad, but it was close.

Hire People Who Will Do Whatever It Takes

Ernest Shackleton, the Arctic explorer, surrounded himself with cheerful, optimistic people. To weed out potential slackers, the explorer only hired people who were willing to tackle any job. He only wanted crewmembers who were hungriest for the job, because they would work harder to keep it.[3] One day as he was about to leave his office, after waiting in vain for candidates whom he had challenged to show up with less than 24 hours' notice, Shackleton was surprised to see a rain-soaked and disheveled man walking through the door. When he learned that this man had immediately left Cornwall for London upon receipt of his telegram, interrupting a trip and rushing through several trains to get there on time, Shackleton hired him on the spot.

When I hire someone, I remember the book *A Message to Garcia*. I'd love to have 300 Lieutenant Rowans working for me. Those employees do whatever it takes to get the job done.

When I interview someone, I look for integrity. I don't want a salesperson who could sell the Brooklyn Bridge. Will Rogers, the great humorist, said that it's nice to be shrewd, but it's better to be ethical. He also said that, "I would rather be the man who bought the Brooklyn Bridge than the one who sold it." We only want employees who are respected for their expertise, not their gift for gab and selling.

The Profile of the Ideal Applicant

I hire people who have a high energy level, who are optimistic and upbeat. Negative people can damage or even destroy a company, regardless of their skill level. After personal experiences with people who are negative, I learned my lesson; all they see are problems, not solutions. Sour employees can bring down everyone around them.

I do expect employees to be loyal to the mission of the company in good times or bad. Elbert Hubbard, who wrote *A Message to Garcia*, said, "An ounce of loyalty is worth a pound of cleverness."[4] I want employees to respect the culture of our firm.

I like Ricardo Semler's approach to hiring. Semler, the author of *Maverick*, advises that the people in charge of hiring should put together a profile of the ideal candidate. The profile describes all of the qualities an applicant should possess. Each requirement is given a weight according to its importance. At Semler's company in Brazil, some factors are not important at all. The corporate culture is to ignore factors such as academic background and personal appearance. Semler says, "Semco abounds with people who lack fancy degrees or Italian suits but are first-class employees nonetheless."[5]

Author Oren Harari discussed Colin Powell's rules for recruiting and promoting. Powell believes in hiring someone based on talent and values, not just the person's resume. Powell looks for qualities such as intelligence, judgment, loyalty, integrity, and a healthy ego.[6]

I surround myself with people who have heart and hope. They remind me of hurdlers at a track meet. Whether the hurdles are low or high, or they knock them over, they finish the race. They may not always finish first, but they finish.

Price Pritchett, chairman of a Dallas-based consulting, training, and publishing firm, advises that people are the crown jewels of a company. He recommends that you should always be on the lookout for talent, whether you have a job opening or not. Pritchett suggests that you supply your human resources department with the names of men and women you've met who demonstrate a high potential.[7]

A Message from Garcia

If you want to build a great company or be part of a great company you must be willing to hire people and work with people who are smarter than you. You must be willing to give credit where credit is due and you must be willing to keep your ego in check. You must be willing to give in to the advice given to you by experts that you have managed to recruit and who have bought into your dream. To build a great company or to be part of a great company you must find and recruit people who possess a high level of energy, people who are optimistic and who know how to rise above obstacles and be resourceful in the execution of their duties, similar to a Lieutenant Rowan.

To build a great company, always be on the lookout for people who possess the character traits and qualities you seek in a person who is a good match for your firm, regardless if they work in your particular industry or not. Integrity, loyalty, intelligence and optimism are traits that can transfer to any industry; find people who possess these traits, convince them of your dream, and try to recruit them. Oftentimes, people who come from outside a particular industry possess a fresh and unique perspective and can bring particularly intriguing and positive insights to a company's performance. In the long run, everyone benefits.

CHAPTER 30

Focus on Your Strengths, Not Your Weaknesses

I DON'T KNOW WHO SAID IT FIRST, BUT I LIKE THE EXPRESSION, "Never try to teach a pig to sing. It wastes your time and annoys the pig."[1]

Unfortunately, it is a fact of life that there are certain fields in which we are unlikely to find success. Although we may accept the premise that a movie character like Rocky can win the heavyweight championship after months of intense training, no one is likely to believe that Rocky could become a great mathematician and win the Nobel Prize in Economics as John Nash did. If you're in your seventies or eighties, it's not likely you'll achieve anything that might require extraordinary or exceptional physical skills, no matter how badly you want it.

As you pursue your passions, it is wise to focus on your strengths, not your weaknesses. John Wooden, whose coaching record at UCLA is unmatched, advised, "Do not permit what you cannot do to interfere with what you can do."[2]

Discover Your Strengths and Your Weaknesses

As you probably realized by now, I'm a big fan of the book by Marcus Buckingham and Donald O. Clifton, *Now, Discover Your*

Strengths. According to this book, all of us are born with some natural talents, and it is essential for you to identify them. Instead of wasting time and energy working harder on your weakest skills, focus on your assets and try to improve them by 20 percent or more. Even if your skills are very strong in one area, you may still have to work further to develop them. Everyone assumes that Michael Jordan's talents are innate and he didn't need to work hard to achieve greatness. As Jordan has said, however, "I've always believed that if you put in the work, the results will come. I don't do things half-heartedly. Because I know if I do, then I can expect half-hearted results."[3]

In many companies, the focus is on finding employees' weaknesses and developing that skill into mediocrity at best. Mediocrity or mere adequacy doesn't cut it in the business world. Buckingham and Clifton point to two assumptions that guide the best managers. These managers believe that "Each person's talents are enduring and unique," and that "Each person's greatest room for growth is in the areas of his or her greatest strength."[4]

At Sterling Financial, we divide responsibilities among the people who are most qualified to handle them. We don't let employees handle duties in the areas where they are weak. We want them working in an area where they can reach superstar level, not where they'll be fortunate to reach mediocrity, adequacy, or just an average level of performance. If an employee isn't a math wiz, that employee will not be working with numbers. Although that person might ultimately be able to do an adequate job, a rapidly growing business needs more than adequate employees. Every entrepreneur needs employees who start out with strengths in certain areas and become even stronger as time progresses and the business grows.

Academy Award-winning director Ron Howard, or Opie Cunningham as Eddie Murphy called him, said in an interview: "I discover what people are good at and create an environment in which they can excel."[5]

Help Your Family Discover Their Strengths

In your personal life as well you should focus on your strengths, not your weaknesses. If your spouse or life partner has great organizational skills, he or she should keep the family organized. Although you can help your children improve on their weaknesses, it's important that they focus on their strengths. If your son's hand-eye coordination isn't nearly as good as his ear for music, focus on his strengths. Focusing on your strengths shouldn't be used as an excuse for failure. As you build your life around your strengths, certain building blocks must be in place. An education is one very important building block.

A Message from Garcia

Find out what your strengths are as a person and pursue those traits or attributes in your career choice. We all have certain things that we are better at than others. One of the keys to success is building upon those strengths as a platform not only for our individual success but also as a member of a company or organization. The most successful people are highly proficient in a particular field; they are experts or specialists at whatever it is they do.

If you don't know what it is you are good at, take any one of the various personality and knowledge tests that are referenced in this book. Put your energy into pursing things at which you have a more natural proficiency and you will not only take the steps toward becoming successful, but will make strides towards achieving personal satisfaction and fulfillment.

PART FIVE

SUCCESS STRATEGY 3: TAKE ACTION

CHAPTER 31

....

Accomplish Something
Every Day

AT THIS POINT, YOU HAVE DETERMINED WHAT YOUR STRENGTHS ARE, you have established a detailed plan to reach your goal, and you are burning with *ganas*. Now comes the time to implement the steps that will move you toward that goal. The third success strategy involves taking action. The power to achieve your dreams comes from knowledge *and* action. Knowledge by itself isn't enough; knowledge and action create a very potent combination. If you really want to achieve your goals, you'll take action and accomplish something every day that helps you to move toward it.

Hopefully, you're doing more to make your dreams come true than buying a lottery ticket. For most people, the journey to success begins with an education. And you can't be a "Rajneesh," the word Jaime Escalante used to describe a student who wants an A in class without doing any work.[1]

Success from the Bottom Up

Callie Khouri, the screenwriter of *Thelma and Louise* and the director of *Divine Secrets of the Ya-Ya Sisterhood,* worked as a waitress in the early 1980s at a Beverly Hills restaurant. She later took a job as a receptionist at a production company. Khouri used that job as a springboard to a career as the producer of music videos. When her *Thelma and Louise* screenplay took off, she parlayed her success into a career as a director.[2]

Ray Kroc started his career at Howard Johnson's diners. At age 52, he mortgaged his house and invested his life savings to buy the exclusive distribution rights to an innovative milk shake maker. Kroc heard about a hamburger stand in San Bernardino that was running eight of these milk shake makers to keep up with demand. Hoping to sell more of the machines, Kroc headed for California. The tiny hamburger restaurant was run by two brothers, Dick and Mac McDonald.[3] Seeing a market for more milk shake makers, Kroc talked them into opening more restaurants and offered to run them. Krok opened his first McDonald's in 1955 in Des Plaines, Illinois, and bought out the McDonald brothers for $2.7 million in 1961. The rest, as we all know, is history.

Develop a Growth Attitude

Most successful people have a growth attitude. I welcome fresh challenges and like to try new activities. It's important for me to make my own decisions and swim against the tide if necessary.

For good or bad, the media have called me a jack of all trades, and I'm not sure they always mean it as a compliment. Regardless, I see it that way because I view myself as having many interests and a desire to achieve success in many areas. When one of your strengths is achievement, you realize that you don't feel good about yourself unless you've achieved something every day, even if it's Sunday.

Some would argue that my desire to accomplish something every day is a bit obsessive. Well, I do admit everyone's sleep requirements are different. You don't have to limit your sleep to six hours per night to accomplish something worthwhile every day. Some presidents, for example, take a nap during the day and still manage to do a great job running the country.

Each New Day Gives You a Fresh Start

Lance Armstrong is one of the greatest cyclists in history and keeps winning important races, despite his having to overcome cancer. As it turns out, Armstrong did not have a happy youth, and when things weren't good Armstrong's mother would tell him, "Well, today is the first day of the rest of your life." Armstrong's mother forced him to focus on the future, not what happened yesterday. Each day, Armstrong pushes forward toward new accomplishments. In 2002, he won the Tour de France again.[4]

"Buzzy" Schwartz, the legendary trader and one of my mentors, advised that you should start each day with a clean emotional slate. You can't let yesterday's defeats carry over and ruin the next day. Yesterday is over, and you must start fresh again. Like Armstrong, Schwartz has far more wins than he has losses.

Granted, not everyone can win the Tour de France or have the acumen to be one of the best traders in America. The concept of accomplishment can be viewed in relative terms and means different things for different people. In some businesses, making the payroll in difficult economic times is a big accomplishment. For some people, feeding their family while struggling from paycheck to paycheck is also a big accomplishment.

Spending time with your children is something you should do every day. That is an accomplishment. Also, helping them learn will not only be a great satisfaction to you, but one of the greatest achievements you can accomplish as a parent and human being.

A Message from Garcia

All great plans require one thing—action. You can talk about something until you're blue in the face, but until you take some action toward achieving your goal, it will be an unfulfilled dream. Once you have defined your dream and established a plan of action, you must take action toward making the dream a reality. The achievement of a dream, depending upon how big or small it is, may take weeks, months, or even years. Your plan should include a timeline and specific goals and steps you must accomplish to achieve your dream. Regularly review your plan to monitor your progress.

It's easy for life to get in the way and sidetrack you from accomplishing your goals, but remain focused on the dream. Regularly consult your action plan and do something every day or every week toward achieving your goals, and you will achieve them. Where possible, you should pursue your dream by approaching it from as many angles as possible and using creative tactics where feasible. Regardless of how many approaches you use, you must actively work toward it regularly to achieve results.

CHAPTER 32

··

To Pursue Your Passion, Find a Good Mentor

WITH THE RIGHT MENTOR, YOU CAN PURSUE YOUR PASSION IN ANY field. Omar Khan was a scrawny teenager when he walked in the office of Buddy Teevens, the Tulane football coach, in 1996. Khan, the son of immigrants from Honduras and India, wanted to learn about football, not the game so much as the business of football, and was willing to start on the ground floor. A Tulane student at the time, Khan volunteered to work for free and was willing to handle any task thrown his way.

The coach had seen others like Khan, or so he thought. Many students begged for work but in the end weren't willing to put in the time because they weren't getting paid. Khan, on the other hand, took on every assignment and became indispensable to the Tulane football program. Khan handled everything from computer projects to travel arrangements to filming practices and games.

In 1996, while still a senior at Tulane, Khan managed to land himself an internship with the New Orleans Saints. As was the case at Tulane, Khan handled any and every project given to him and, in early 1998, he was hired as a full-time employee of the Saints. One of his mentors at the Saints was Terry O'Neill, who helped the football team with salary cap issues. Khan helped to research the contracts that O'Neill negotiated. By age 21, Khan was negotiating some of the smaller contracts. When O'Neill left the Saints, Coach Jim Hazlett hired Khan to be his administrative assistant.

On his twenty-fourth birthday, Khan was hired away from the Saints by the Pittsburgh Steelers. At age 25, he became the youngest business coordinator in the National Football League. Khan rose to become the Steelers' lead negotiator, in addition to coordinating the team's travel plans and managing their salary cap. He has negotiated some of the largest contracts in Steelers' history, while keeping the club's salary cap under control. Today, Khan manages a salary cap that is in excess of $71 million.[1]

Chris Janson is also pursuing his passion, thanks to his mentor. Stedman Graham, Oprah Winfrey's boyfriend, talked about receiving a letter from Janson, a Marquette University student. Janson offered to work for free in Graham's entertainment and sports marketing consulting firm. Janson's persistence and willingness to work for free convinced Graham to hire him as an intern.[2]

Along with the contacts he made while working at the firm, Janson made a big impression on Graham. After a brief time in a nonpaying intern position, Graham thought enough of Janson to hire him as an employee. In addition to his paycheck, Janson is getting invaluable experience in the areas of marketing, event planning, logistical coordination, and every aspect of the business.[3]

Charles Krauthammer found himself an extraordinary mentor. Dr. Krauthammer wouldn't have become a Pulitzer Prize–winning newspaper columnist without his mentor, Dr. Hermann Lisco. When he was a freshman at Harvard Medical School, Krauthammer was paralyzed in a serious accident. At the time of the accident, Dr. Lisco was the associate dean. Lisco convinced professors at Harvard to give the paralyzed student bedside lectures. Because Krauthammer was unable to write at the time, Lisco also persuaded the professors to give the injured student oral exams. Lisco even arranged for Krauthammer's rehabilitation to take place at a Harvard teaching hospital so he wouldn't fall behind in his studies. Krauthammer used a wheelchair to go on rounds with his fellow classmates.

Thanks to Lisco, Krauthammer finished his medical degree. He became chief resident in psychiatry at Massachusetts General

Hospital. He later became a science advisor to the Carter administration and a speechwriter for Walter Mondale. In the 1980s, Krauthammer turned to writing and won that Pulitzer Prize.[4]

You'll Never Find a Mentor With a Bad Attitude

Psychologist Carole Kanchier points out that your attitude can limit your options. Having a growth attitude opens up a world of opportunities.[5]

Dr. Kanchier suggests that you ask yourself the following questions: Do I welcome criticism as a way to grow? Do I expect good things to happen? Do I enjoy a challenge and a sense of achievement? Do I accept responsibility for my failures and successes? Do I prefer activities I'm familiar with to the ones I never tried? Would I take a job I don't like for the prestige and money?

Many experts say that if you do what you love, the money will follow. Realistically, that won't always happen, but it shouldn't dissuade you from pursuing your passions. Teachers aren't making huge salaries, but their job has enormous implications for society and humanity. If you have a passion for teaching, pursue that route, even if other careers might offer better salaries.

Whatever your passion is, you must find someone who has already achieved what you want and learn from him or her. Try to build a relationship with that person so you can learn directly from him or her even if it means working for free. Mentors can do more than just teach you how to succeed in a particular area. Mentors can help you avoid the mistakes they made along the way, which gives you a huge advantage.

It helps to be realistic when approaching someone to be your mentor. You'll have better luck with someone who's achieved success in your community rather than someone who is a well-known national success in that field. When searching for a mentor, it helps to have some type of connection to that person. Perhaps a mutual friend can introduce you, or you could have something in common—a passion for horses, baseball, or vegetarian diets.

Although the best advice will come from your mentor, you also should develop expertise on you own. Become an expert in the field that fascinates you, and learn as much as you can. Make yourself indispensable to those around you, like Khan, and you will succeed.[6]

My Introduction to Mentoring

My father introduced me to the concept of mentoring. Dr. Charles Huffnagel, a top heart surgeon, who treated Presidents Eisenhower and Kennedy, was his mentor. In addition to being a mentor to my father, Dr. Huffnagel is my godfather and I was named after him.

My passion is for the financial services business. I first became intrigued by the financial services field while working as a White House Fellow. One of my bosses was John C. Whitehead, who influenced my decision to embark on a career in financial services. As I mentioned earlier, I studied how he ran Goldman Sachs and utilized this approach in running my company, Sterling Financial. Another of my mentors in the financial services field was Martin "Buzzy" Schwartz, who taught me about trading stocks, futures, and options. Schwartz was a renowned Wall Street trader who was profiled in Barron's and in Jack Schwager's national bestseller, *Market Wizards.*[7] I worked with Schwartz when he was writing his own book, *Pit Bull: Lessons From Wall Street's Champion Trader,*[8] and I'd talk with him at length about his success strategies.

I sought out Schwartz as my mentor after reading about him in 1987. We were both living in Boca Raton, which helped make the connection easier. Another common denominator was that he was in the Marine Corps, and I had been in the Marine Corps staff command. When we ultimately formed a partnership, we decided on the name Leatherneck Partners. Our venture was a hedge fund and you couldn't find a better partner in that business than Schwartz. He taught me what it takes to consistently make money in the stock market.

Schwartz helped me hone in on the four success strategies. He believed in dreaming big, having a well-thought out plan, taking action, and persevering. Schwartz taught me that you have to work twice as hard as anyone else to be successful. It's a lot more fun to work hard when you're learning something new and you like what you're doing. Schwartz saw the market unfold in slow motion and reacted quicker than anyone to opportunities. I once saw him go two weeks without losing money on a trade. He must have made over 250 trades.

Your Mentor's Career
May Not Be as Glamorous as You Think

Mentoring is a good way to find out if a career is as glamorous up close as it is from afar. Mentoring helps you see the good, the bad, and the ugly of the field that excites you. It helps you separate the dream from the reality. And if the bad far outweighs the good, you might decide to reevaluate whether this is something you really want.

For example, from afar, broadcasting seems to be a glamorous and exciting career. If you intern at a radio or television station, however, you will come to learn that you're in for a great deal of hard work. Beginners in the broadcasting field often work 18-hour days. Even as you build up seniority, you'll be working odd hours and will find yourself working on holidays. It becomes a trudge, a routine, and a bore, as do so many jobs beyond the glare of the exciting spotlights. Do you know what time disc jockeys and news reporters get up in the morning? Usually between 3:00 and 4:00 A.M. This type of schedule can wear you down and tarnish the excitement of any profession.

Law students and lawyers find out quickly that the legal profession isn't the way it is portrayed on television. Most legal work takes place outside the dramatic setting of a courtroom. It is the rare exception that a courtroom trial is even remotely as exciting as an episode of *Law and Order*. Mentoring with a lawyer or interning in a law firm before applying for or even attending law school might save you three years of incredibly hard work, and quite possibly save you or your parents a great deal of tuition money.

My partnership with Buzzy Schwartz only lasted three months. I learned I wasn't cut out to be a trader. It's much like being in combat with bazookas shooting at you every minute of every day. I came to realize that I wanted to lead an organization and that being a broker/dealer was much more appealing to me.

Mentoring in Government Service

The White House Fellows program is one of the best mentoring programs in the world. Each Fellow is assigned to the executive office of the president, to the vice president, or to a cabinet-level secretary for one year. All attend private lunches with White House officials, cabinet-level secretaries, top military officers, members of Congress, heads of state, and members of the media. You get to meet these leaders, frequently in an informal setting, and learn a lot from them. In fact, in President George W. Bush's Administration, former White House Fellows include Secretary of State Colin Powell and Secretary of Labor Elaine Chao. Dr. Donna Shalala, the former head of the Department of Health and Human Services who is now the president of the University of Miami, understood the value of teaching White House Fellows about government and leadership. When she came to a cabinet-level meeting, Shalala often said, "Hey, I brought my White House Fellow. Where's yours?"

Mentoring has been a pet project of Governor Jeb Bush in Florida. In 1999, Bush created the Governor's Mentoring Initiative. Since the program was established, about 116,000 people have volunteered as mentors.

Bush himself has been mentoring a seventh-grader at Augusta Raa Middle School in Tallahassee, and helps the boy with his schoolwork. Having the governor as a mentor has motivated the child to get better grades. It was reported that Governor Bush's help really came in handy when the boy was studying Central American history. Governor Bush's father had firsthand experience with the Nicaraguan Contras as vice-president and president.[9]

A Teacher Can Be a Mentor You'll Never Forget

Teachers can often be the mentors who help a child pursue his or her passion. I witnessed this firsthand growing up. My mother was a teacher and she was also a mentor to many children, including me.

An interesting thing happened recently to both me and my mother, which really shows the impact a teacher can have on students' lives. In 2001, many years after my mother retired from teaching and after Sterling Financial was named the fastest-growing privately held firm in the state of Florida, I was invited to Panama for a private reception in honor of my accomplishments in the United States. Of course, for such an event, my mother came along. As we were ushered through the presidential palace, we approached three women who were just in the anteroom of the president's office. These three women fawned over my mother in a way that reminded me of the identification of a rock star on a street.

These women used to be students of my mother's. They remembered her as one of the best teachers they ever had, and I can assure you they were far more impressed with her accomplishments than with mine. My mother taught me that practical lessons go a lot farther than theoretical ones. She was able to put her nursing background at Georgetown to good use and teach practical lessons to her students. For her science classes, she got my father to donate cows' brains and pigs' hearts from his medical laboratory, so her students could dissect them. Years later, my mother's students remembered those experiences fondly and spoke glowingly about how much they learned in her class.

A Message from Garcia

Over the years, you'll spend a large part of your life at work, so find something that you love to do. Finding a mentor in a particular field in which you have an interest can help you achieve personal satisfaction and professional success. Why not learn the mistakes others have made so you don't make them yourself?

You may find that the field you are interested in is right up your alley, or you may find out that it really is something that you do not want to pursue. Either way, the experience will prove valuable. Finding a mentor can take weeks, months, possibly even years, depending upon where you live and the profession or career in which you have an interest. Finding a mentor might require you to work for free. This may be difficult, especially if you are pursuing a new career track later in your adult working life. If you can manage this, the long-term rewards of having a mentor can be great, even if it may cost you financially at first. The experience you gain in the field you love, or think you love, is worth far more than any paycheck you might get in a job you presently might dread or one that you may discover you don't like in the future. Finding a mentor can help you avoid these types of situations and allow you to refine and redefine what your dream is and discover what you may want to do next.

CHAPTER 33

Separate the Real Role Models from the Artificial Ones

YOU CAN PURSUE YOUR PASSIONS BY FINDING A GOOD MENTOR. YOU can pursue the goal of being a better person by finding a good role model, and in turn, being a good role model yourself.

Although some athletes are excellent role models, you should look for qualities beyond the ability to dribble a basketball or throw a football. I admire athletes who finished their college degree instead of dropping out and taking the cash that comes with a pro contract. I'd be much more inclined to view the athlete who drops out as a role model if he or she went back to school during the off-season. Either way, if they set the example of getting an education, I can live with them being paid 100 times more than a public school teacher makes in a year. After all, they're pursuing their passion, they give children who look up to them some sense of responsibility, and they are making a good living at what they do.

Mike Haynes is an athlete I believe we all can admire. Haynes, a member of the Pro Football Hall of Fame and one of the best defensive backs to ever play the game, was drafted in the first round by the New England Patriots in 1976. He dropped out of college, but finished his degree in 1980. Haynes worked every off-season for 14 years to prepare for life after football. Both on the field and off, Haynes set goals and objectives for himself. Haynes is now an executive with the Callaway Golf Company.[1]

Regardless of our ethnicity or racial background, there are role models for all of us. In President Bush's administration alone, we see great role models that represent a wide range of diversity. There's Secretary of State Colin Powell and National Security Advisor Condoleezza Rice, both African-Americans. Transportation Secretary Norman Minetta is a Japanese American, Labor Secretary Elaine Chao was born in Taiwan, Energy Secretary Spencer Abraham is a Lebanese American, and Secretary of Housing and Urban Development Mel Martinez was born in Cuba.

Role Models in Our Schools

More often than not, the real role models are in our schools, not on the football field, up on the movie screen, or in government. In my mind, schoolteachers are the true stars of our society. Jaime Escalante is a magnificent role model and has been called the best teacher in America. I admired Escalante long before I met him. When Escalante taught at Garfield High School, drug dealers were the role models for some of his students. The people selling drugs had money and power, and this was what the students respected. Escalante sent the message that education is a far better route to success.

In February 2002, President George W. Bush appointed me to the White House Initiative on Educational Excellence for Hispanic Americans. Coincidentally, when I was first named to the Florida Board of Education, I gave videotapes of the movie based on Escalante's experiences, *Stand and Deliver*, to other members serving with me to illustrate the importance of the task ahead of us. I was honored when I learned later that I would be working with Escalante on the commission.

Thousands of people have fond memories of Marva Collins, whose passion is educating children. She believes strongly in staying true to the Latin meaning of teacher, which is to lead and draw out. Collins is determined to never lose one child. She has trained over 30,000 teachers and touched the lives of millions of children.[2]

Teachers like Marva Collins help children to find new directions. A kind word of encouragement can motivate children to do more than they might have ever dreamed was possible. Teachers can open up a world of possibilities for a child.

David M. Shribman interviewed people from all walks of life. Everyone he talked with had an anecdote about a teacher who played an important role in his or her life. Whether the person was a good student or a bad one, and no matter what occupation they were in, all of them had a teacher who made a big difference in who they are today.

In the preface to his book *I Remember My Teacher*, Shribman put a refreshing slant on an old saying. Shribman said, "Those who can, do. Those who teach, do more."[3]

Role Models for Our Children

Cheryl K. Olson, of the Harvard Medical School Center for Mental Health, offers this advice on how to raise a child with an upbeat spirit. She recommends that parents encourage their children to find a bright spot in their day. If a child hates one particular subject, encourage him or her to focus on the ones that are enjoyable. Olson also advised that parents should stop children from taking one single negative event and turning it into an awful generalization.[4]

Parents should also have role models such as someone at work who handles difficult situations gracefully. Perhaps your role model is a neighbor who finds time in his or her busy schedule to do community service, or a buddy who passes up drinks with the guys to coach the soccer team or little league baseball. As you strive to be a better role model, remember the six essential qualities— sincerity, personal integrity, humility, courtesy, wisdom, and charity—that Dr. William Menninger identified as the key to success.[5]

The Soft Bigotry of Low Expectations

Many people believe in "dumbing down" our schools, so children will have high self-esteem. But true achievement, whether in sports, academics, or any other area, produces true self-esteem. Hard work is what brought self-esteem to the students in Jaime Escalante's classes. No one lowered the bar on the AP calculus exam so they could feel a sense of self-esteem. Their achievement taught the children, their parents, and the community that they were able to go on to college, and many of them did.

The first major piece of legislation that President George W. Bush passed was his "No Child Left Behind" education bill. President Bush's belief that every child in America can learn often collides with what he calls the "soft bigotry of low expectations." The idea that some people have low expectations of certain ethnic groups is simply unacceptable. This may be "soft" bigotry, but it's still bigotry. Low expectation means that certain children just get shuffled through the system. They're generally inner-city kids, minorities, and kids whose parents may not speak English as a first language. It's so much easier to walk into a classroom full of children that are hard to educate and just say, "see you later, we're just going to promote you to the next grade and move you through the system." Those days have got to end.

Hispanic children are in serious trouble. More than a third drop out of high school before they graduate. I hate to call the kids who fail to graduate "dropouts," because I don't believe it is their fault. As a policy maker on the state and federal level, I have seen that school personnel have low expectations of Hispanic children, and thus these children are not encouraged to think about college at an early age. Only a small percentage of Hispanic children go to preschool and other early education programs, which hampers their progress. This is compounded by tracking Hispanic children into non-academic classes, the lack of teachers who speak Spanish, and isolation into resource-poor schools. Further, the assets a child brings into the classroom, such as a second language, are not universally valued; and the active participation of parents in the education of their children is not facilitiated by school administrators.

A Message from Garcia
••

The best role models aren't usually star athletes, TV icons, rock stars, or supermodels. The best role models are all around us and in front of us every day. They are parents and teachers. Parents are children's first role models. Parents should make sure that children respect their teachers because teachers can be the most influential role model a child can have in their life. Parents and teachers should always promote the idea that getting a good education is the best way to succeed. Role models should also be individuals who demonstrate qualities that contribute to good character development, who have a sense of ethics and morals, and who believe that success is more than just what is in your bank account, that what matters is what is inside you as a person. Qualities such as honesty and integrity are essential in the healthy and positive development of people of all ages.

Think about the people you admire, whether it's Dr. Martin Luther King Jr. or a neighbor who always lends a helping hand. Ask yourself what it is about them that triggered your admiration. Are they kind and compassionate? Do they give of themselves, their time, their money and resources to help someone or a worthy cause? Try to cultivate those qualities in yourself and in turn, you should become the best role model you can be.

CHAPTER 34

Keep a War Book

STERLING FINANCIAL GROUP OF COMPANIES IS A HISPANIC-OWNED Minority Business Enterprise founded in September 1997. In August 2002, the company was recognized as the fastest growing Hispanic-owned company in the United States, according to *Hispanic Business* magazine. We were also named the 8th fastest growing privately held company in the United States by *Inc* magazine in its prestigious "Inc 500" list in October 2002, and identified, for two consecutive years, as the fastest growing private company in the State of Florida.

Our goal is to become the leading Hispanic-owned financial services firm catering to U.S. institutional investors as well as the underserved and fragmented Hispanic corporate and retail market. We generate revenue from four primary sources including proprietary research, institutional sales and trading, wealth management and investment banking.

Our proprietary research best exemplifies our philosophy of providing unbiased product offerings. Early on, we recognized the need for independent research that conventional investment banks have failed to provide due to their reliance on research as a means of supporting investment banking fee business. Our research stands on the merits of the tangible returns it provides to investors.

Our institutional sales and trading group encompasses both equities and fixed income divisions. Our traders provide institutions with quality trade execution, while our institutional sales force serves as an effective conduit for the distribution of our equity and fixed income research product. Our fixed income team has developed competencies in a wide variety of debt instruments while our equity sales and trading effort has acquired specialized expertise in emerging growth sectors including healthcare and technology.

Our wealth management business is comprised of our domestic and international private client service group and our emerging asset management business. We have a growing international presence, and currently boast 62 offices in many of the key U.S. and Hispanic markets and in five Latin American countries.

Our investment banking group consists of multilingual, multicultural professionals with international expertise. We believe we have assembled a team that will enable us to compete effectively in the traditional U.S. market while also allowing us to meet the special needs of Hispanic-owned and focused companies as well as Latin American companies that we see as being beneficiaries of the region's economic convergence with the U.S. I have employees and independent contractors throughout the United States and in seven countries. Even if I wanted to, I couldn't be a micromanager. Nonetheless, I still need to monitor how the company is doing and what areas need my attention. The *war book* helps me keep tabs on what's going on in my company on a daily basis in offices throughout the world.

The *war book* is a compilation of the daily reports I receive from managers at each of Sterling's worldwide offices. It helps keep the lines of communication open and makes it possible for me to know immediately if there's a problem that demands my attention. By keeping the lines of communication open with my people, they know I care. Without daily communication, employees and contractors at remote locations would feel isolated and wouldn't recognize how important their role is in the company's success.

Right outside my office door is my Global Relationship Team. They're actually what I call my "internal auditing team." The team is my version of Internal Affairs, whose mission is to find quality and service problems. The Global Relationship Team maintains contact with each and every office each day. Before the Global Relationship Team was in place, I only found out what the problems were when one of my financial advisors complained.

In my business, the financial advisors are my customers, not the end user. We've grown so rapidly because the advisors want to be a part of the Sterling team, since it gives them access to our exceptional research. They pass this information along to their clients, who are investors throughout the world. The brokers share our recommendations with their clients.

The Global Relationship Team calls each financial advisor every day. Team members ask two questions of the broker. The first is whether there's anything we're doing wrong. The second is what can we do that we're not doing now that can help make your clients happier. The results of those conversations wind up in the *war book*. As you might suspect, the idea of keeping a *war book* came from my military background. When you're an aide to a general, he or she comes in every day and looks at a briefing book. It has the general's schedule and reports from division commanders. The *war book* serves another purpose. It keeps employees on their toes because they know I'll be checking on them.

You Need More Than a Day Planner or Palm Pilot to Succeed

Your career and your business may not require a *war book*. Whether you're a manager, entrepreneur, or an employee, you should keep a journal or diary with the status of pending projects. You need to know who's leading the charge and also check to make sure those projects are moving forward. Review it daily and weekly so projects and assignments don't slip between the cracks.

The war book can also help you keep on top of the million little things that can turn into big problems. My father-in-law,

Seymour Holtzman, taught me that the devil is in the details. To be a businessperson, you need to know every detail of how your business works, and read every document that crosses your desk. Holtzman once lost $2 million in a real estate deal because of one word in the contract. Even though he isn't a lawyer, Holtzman reads every word in contracts and makes lawyers explain paragraphs if he's unsure of their purpose.

Even if you don't run a company, you can have your own *war book*. It would then look more like a success journal. Write down all the projects that you're working on, and keep track of your progress toward finishing them. You can also keep tabs on your personal goals the same way. In the success journal, write down your dreams and how you plan to accomplish them. Look at them each day and write down what you've done toward making them a reality.

A Message from Garcia

In your battle to achieve success, keeping a war book can turn you into a victorious field marshal. If you already run a company, it will allow you to keep tabs on your employee's projects. If you're a manager in a large company, your own war book will help you keep track of the status of all essential projects that every one of your employees is working on. When your boss asks you a question about the status of something, the war book helps you lay out what's going on in your organization.

Even if you don't own a business or manage anyone, you should keep a war book, a diary, or a success journal to help keep track of your progress toward your goals. You'll quickly see if there are days where you wasted your time and didn't even take a baby step toward achieving something you have desired to strive for. You'll also be able to determine and analyze the most productive moves you made, and learn from your current experience.

CHAPTER 35

....

Time Is Your Enemy
or
Time Is Your Friend

MY FATHER-IN-LAW, SEYMOUR HOLTZMAN, TAUGHT ME THAT WHEN analyzing a deal, time is either your enemy or your friend. If time is your friend, you can drag things out in a negotiation. If time is your enemy, you must act quickly.

When time is your ally, you don't feel pressured to make decisions without all of the information you need and you're able to complete a thorough analysis of the situation. One of the biggest problems facing entrepreneurs, however, is that they frequently must make decisions with only a small percentage of the information they need. If the entrepreneur waits until he or she has 90 percent of the necessary information the window of opportunity may be lost.

I've faced situations like this in running my business. I had heard that Merrill Lynch was closing its office in Greece. I saw an opportunity for Sterling Financial to jump into that market. Within a day, I was on a plane to Greece to recruit Merrill Lynch's people and open an office there. Using lawyers in Greece, London, and the United States, we managed to file all of the necessary paperwork and open an office in two weeks. Even though time was clearly our enemy, we utilized every hour of every day engaging the efforts of people in different countries to make sure that we were able to close this deal. We were able to open an office in Athens with some great people and quickly establish a presence in a new international market in which we had an interest.

On another occasion, I was having lunch with a competitor who was interested in buying our company. During our chat, he mentioned another firm that his company was thinking of buying. If he could buy the other company, so could I. I called the owner of that firm and convinced him to sell his operation to us. Three days later we had a deal, and I virtually doubled my sales force right away.

If time is on your side, you don't have to make purchasing decisions on the spot. You should always get multiple bids on almost everything. We were in the market for a new phone system that cost about $19,000. As we got bids, I found out from one vendor that a used phone system was much cheaper and would adequately meet our needs. Instead of just buying that used phone system, I followed my father-in-law's advice and got multiple bids again. In the end, we got the used phone system for much less than the first vendor was quoting.

When time is your friend, you can afford to walk away from the table if you're not getting the deal you want. Often, the other party will come back later with a better offer. To get the best deal, you may have to walk away from it, even if you've spent six months at the negotiating table. The other side may have so much time and money invested in the deal, they may blink and agree to the terms still in dispute.

A Message from Garcia

Make time your friend by remaining clear about what must be accomplished before a particular deadline comes. Set your own cut-off dates and firmly stick to them. In addition, remember to leave time for the inevitable mistakes or snafus that can throw a monkey wrench into the most perfectly set plans.

Strategic planning can help you make sure that time is your friend rather than your enemy. Bad planners naturally make time their enemy. They're always behind the eight ball instead of being ahead of the curve.

Time can work to your advantage if you are proactive in your planning, mapping out the specific steps to be taken toward achieving a particular goal or meeting deadlines on a project. If time is on your side, take all the time you can to reach a good decision. You can do this by consulting people who can add something valuable to the decision-making process. If possible, reach out to the necessary constituents who may be affected by the final decision so everyone feels that they were part of the decision-making process.

CHAPTER 36

Develop Leadership Skills

YOU CAN BE A LEADER, NO MATTER WHAT POSITION YOU'RE IN. There are privates in the armed forces who demonstrate leadership skills. The chain of command doesn't change, but the private inspires the soldiers around him or her.

Even if you're a civilian, there's a lot to learn from the combat model of leadership. In his book *The New Art of the Leader*, William A. Cohen sets forth the combat model and the eight universal laws of leadership. According to Cohen, a Ph.D. and retired major general in the Air Force Reserve, these laws apply whether you're leading troops into battle or leading a Parent Teachers Association meeting.[1]

1. Maintain absolute integrity, which is the foundation of all leadership.
2. Know your stuff.
3. Declare your expectations.
4. Show uncommon commitment.
5. Expect positive results.
6. Take care of your people.
7. Put duty before self.
8. Get out in front.

I've incorporated the Air Force Academy values into my business model. The Air Force Academy's mission statement focuses on producing leaders who possess forthright integrity. They accept responsibility and avoid passing the buck. The Academy's mission statement also stresses the need to be selfless and committed to duty. Graduates should be decisive and disciplined. These are qualities you want from the people in your business as well.[2]

You Can Lead from the Bottom or the Top

One way to begin developing your leadership skills is by expressing your views and having an opinion on a current event or on a hot topic of debate within your company or organization. Share your thoughts and opinions on significant issues facing the company, provided they are well thought out and offered without malice.

Authors Pat Heim and Elwood Chapman argue in their book *Learning to Lead* that there are three sources of leadership power. Those sources are personality power, role power, and knowledge power. The ability to lead does not necessarily spring from the position you hold. Knowledge power is an important source of leadership power and anyone can empower himself or herself with knowledge.

Even if you are at the lowest level of an organization, your personality might enable you to take the lead on certain assignments. According to Heim and Chapman, some individuals have mental characteristics and traits that make others want to follow them. Perhaps it's your sense of fairness, decisiveness, positive attitude, willingness to accept responsibility, or some other characteristic that others see in you. It is easier to accept as a leader someone who demonstrates these characteristics.[3]

Napoleon Hill offers ways to assemble an attractive personality. You can do this by improving the different aspects of your personality, such as flexibility, courtesy, sense of humor, versatility, and humility. A positive mental attitude is the most important element of an attractive personality.[4]

William Sonnenschein made that cogent point in his book *The Diversity Toolkit*, when he observed that, "When people feel respected and know their input will be appreciated and potentially used, they will take on leadership roles even if they are not in leadership positions."[5] When people take on a leadership role, they increase their capacity to lead. As renowned historian Cyril Falls said, "The very exercise of leadership fosters a capacity for it."[6]

In sports, you'll see leaders of every kind. There are players with forceful personalities who motivate their teammates. There are also players who lead by example. They don't talk much, but the determination shown by their actions in turn motivates their teammates to try harder.

Strive to Be a Leader, Not a Manager

The best managers also can be leaders. They push the envelope and move beyond the parameters of their job description. Instead of waiting for explicit instructions, they develop novel approaches for getting the job done. They try new ideas without asking their boss for approval.

Colin Powell defines leadership this way: "Leadership is the art of accomplishing more than the science of management says is possible." [7] Powell also said that the leader's role is to generate organizational consensus.[8] Powell believes that a leader must be crystal clear about the direction in which the organization is going. A leader must communicate his or her vision in compelling terms. The leader works on being inclusive and seeks a personal commitment from every member of his or her team. In the end, although the leader seeks consensus, he or she can only do so much compromising and must move forward decisively.[9] Along the same lines, Martin Luther King Jr. said, "A genuine leader is not a searcher for consensus but a molder of consensus."[10]

Bring Out the Leadership Qualities In Your Children

As a parent, it is important for you to nurture and cultivate leadership qualities in your children. First, you must understand your children's personality, disposition, and temperament. Watch how they react in stressful situations, and offer suggestions for them to handle the pressure more appropriately. Teach them the organizational skills that will serve them well throughout their lifetime. Nurture their independence, instead of just plain nurturing them for way too long.

Giving your children too much has a way of sucking the motivation right out of them. When I learned fly-fishing from my grandfather, he gave me a nickel for each successful cast. Those nickels meant 100 times more to me than if he had just given me a dollar. It helped me learn about the financial rewards that come with success.

I've always believed in the old Chinese proverb that says, "Give a man a fish and he'll eat for a day. Teach a man to fish, and he'll eat for a lifetime."[11]

A Message from Garcia

Many successful people are natural born leaders. Some rise to the top of an organization due to their passion, knowledge, or commitment to a project or endeavor. Or perhaps they have the vision to advance a new idea, such as starting a company or becoming an advocate for a cause. To be a leader, you must be fair, decisive, and action-oriented. You must have a willingness to accept responsibility and a desire to work with others to achieve something that you could not achieve by yourself. Leaders are flexible, courteous and respectful of the opinions of others, and consider all points of view before making a decision and setting a course of action. You can also enhance your own leadership skills by studying the great leaders in history; many lessons can be learned from leaders of all walks of life, lessons that you can apply to yourself and your own circumstances.

Even if you are not a natural born leader you can develop and cultivate your own leadership skills. Seek out leadership opportunities. Volunteer for assignments that will allow you to take the lead on projects and that put you in a position to take charge, to delegate responsibility and encourage people to achieve things that they normally might not seek to achieve on their own. You would be surprised that these opportunities are all around you if you just look for them. When I was at the Air Force Academy, I volunteered for leadership courses at the U.S. Military Academy at West Point and the U.S. Navel Academy at Annapolis. I tried to learn about leadership on a national level by becoming a White House Fellow. In the State of Florida, I joined a year-long program called Leadership Florida with seventy leaders from around the state to further cultivate and fine-tune our leadership skills and learn more about our great state. In business there are two national leadership programs that you should consider joining: The Young President's Organization (YPO) and The Executive Committee (TEC). Each organization gives you an opportunity to interact with business leaders in your community and learn a great deal that you can apply to your business or personal life.

CHAPTER 37

To Communicate Effectively, Make Complicated Issues Understandable and Relevant

WHETHER YOU'RE THE LEADER OF THE FREE WORLD, THE LEADER OF a company, or a parent, you need the ability to take complicated issues and make them understandable. We all seem to be busier than ever and distracted by a general inundation of information. Leaders must be able to cut through the clutter that competes for our attention and convey a message that is clear and relevant.

Bill Bennett believes that people do not and will not care about something you have to say unless you make it understandable. He also shows why the issue should be important to whomever you address. Bennett excels at taking issues like education or the war on drugs and showing the American people why they should care about them. He is masterful at illustrating how issues impact us and how they touch our lives.

Know What You're Going to Say Before You Say It

Preparation is the key to communicating effectively. In the courtroom, the lawyer who prepares meticulously stands a better chance of winning. Even when you talk with your children about important issues, you should go over what you're planning to say in advance. Otherwise, when you're child asks why, you'll be answering, "Because I said so."

It is the rare individual who can articulate his or her position on important issues without preparation. Abraham Lincoln was a great orator, but historian William Lee Miller found that he was not a very good extemporaneous speaker. Before debating Stephen Douglas, Lincoln spent days studying his opponent's speeches. Lincoln also studied the speeches of other senators and read newspapers from across the country. He came to the debate fully prepared and performed well.[1]

Retired Admiral James Stockdale, a war hero who survived almost eight years in a North Vietnamese prisoner-of-war camp, is best remembered for his poor showing in the televised 1992 vicepresidential debate. Stockdale was running on Ross Perot's ticket and learned at the last minute that he would be participating in the debate. Unlike other candidates who spend weeks, sometimes months preparing for a debate, he was not prepped on any of the questions that might be thrown at him. Consequently, he could not articulate a clear position on any of the issues. According to the experts, Stockdale lost the debate, although no one can question his intelligence, bravery, or character. Stockdale correctly has pointed out that "Character is permanent and issues are transient," but that didn't help him win that evening. To communicate effectively, you must be fully prepared or your message will be lost.[2]

Keep It Simple

Written communication must be every bit as clear and under-standable as that presented orally. When I was writing about complex issues like the fight against terrorism or the war on drugs, my bosses had no use for analysis that made a complex subject even more complicated. If you can't explain something in simple terms, you really don't understand the subject. Take a position and support it with necessary facts or figures, but keep it simple!

When you give a speech, always know what your message is. Too many speakers are so busy telling jokes and rambling on about extraneous topics that they forget what their message is. President Dwight Eisenhower said that you should be able to fit the message of any speech on the inside cover of a match-book.[3]Thomas Jefferson also believed in the value of being suc-cinct. Jefferson said, "The most valuable of talents is to never use two words when one will do."[4]

Author Stephen King's writing style is a wee bit different from Thomas Jefferson's, but he offers great advice on how to write. King recommends using the first words that come to mind, instead of more complicated language. For instance, the word "tip" is preferable to "gratuity" or "emolument." King suggests using short sentences because short and simple statements have more power. In addition, he stays away from adverbs. In the sen-tence, "The man closed the door firmly," the adverb "firmly" doesn't add much to the sentence. King also advises using the active tense. As an example, you would say, "They carried the body from the kitchen." "The body was carried from the kitchen," is an example of the passive tense.[5]

A Message from Garcia

Speak simply and clearly. Employ this premise in your writing as well. Know what you are going to say before you speak. And when communicating your message in writing, be sure to articulate your point with clarity and brevity. When dealing with complicated issues, be sure to distill them into simple-to-understand points and make them as relevant as possible to your intended target audience.

Complicated issues demand simple and straightforward discussions to resolve them. Difficult questions deserve well-thought-out answers, not off-the-cuff responses. The successful presentation of facts, whether complex or not, requires preparation. The better prepared you are to advocate a particular position, whether you're arguing in court or making a case to the Board of Directors, the stronger your communication will be. To be successful in advocating a cause or position, you need to demonstrate your understanding of the issues instead of relying on emotion and rhetoric. Even when speaking with your children, you're better off using logic and legitimate arguments, instead of falling back on your authority as a parent.

....

CHAPTER 38

Successful People Have the Courage to Disagree When Necessary

FILM PRODUCER SAMUEL GOLDWYN SAID, "I DON'T WANT ANY YES men around me. I want everyone to tell me the truth, even though it costs him his job."[1] I get a laugh out of Goldwyn's quip, and I don't like yes men or women either. My attitude is like that of Ernest Shackleton, the Antarctic explorer. In choosing a crew, Shackleton selected people who demonstrated loyalty but weren't yes men. As Morell and Capparell's book *Shackleton's Way* points out, today's leaders deal with employees who are "better educated, well traveled, more ambitious and worldlier than ever before."[2] For that reason, it is imperative to establish a brand of leadership that values your employees opinions. Leaders should follow what Morell and Capparell dubbed "Shackleton's way," an approach marked by humor, generosity, intelligence, strength, and compassion. They call it "business with a human face."[3]

No one's ever lost their job in my company by disagreeing with me; I encourage everyone around me to think for themselves, and to learn from their own mistakes.[4] I want to be surrounded by people who are willing to take a different position than mine, instead of telling me I'm right all the time.

You must always stand up for what you believe in; if you hold an appointed government position you should remember that if you are not willing to walk away from power, then you have no power. This basic truth was tested on me when the University of Michigan Law School's admission policy of trying to attain a diverse student body was challenged all the way up to the U.S. Supreme Court. The President and the Governor of Florida, leaders whom I deeply respect—and for whom I worked—submitted briefs to the Court urging them to declare those admission practices unconstitutional.

Although both the President and the Governor of Florida are deeply committed to diversity in every sense of the word, they believe that racially neutral means exist that can bring diversity to campuses. As Governors, they both adopted ground-breaking "percentage plans" that automatically admit a certain portion of high school graduates to universities regardless of race. While these race-neutral plans have worked well in Florida and Texas, I do not believe that they would work in every state. In my opinion, these plans also have limitations with more selective universities and graduate schools. In judging a person's merit to attend a public university, which trains tomorrows leaders, I feel one has to look beyond grades and scores on standardized tests to include a rigorous analysis of the diverse facets of an individual's character.

For this reason I directed that my company join the "Fortune 500" brief of leading American businesses supporting the University of Michigan. Over sixty Fortune 500 companies, including Boeing, Coca-Cola, G.E., Intel, Microsoft, Procter & Gamble, and many others argued to the U.S. Supreme Court that a well educated, diverse workforce, comprised of people who have learned to work productively with individuals from a multitude of racial, ethnic, religious, and cultural backgrounds, is necessary to maintain America's competitiveness in the increasingly diverse and interconnected world economy. Of the sixty-five companies that joined the brief, Sterling Financial Group of Companies was one of only three firms that was not on the Fortune 500 list. Apart from the Fortune 500 brief, more than sixty national organizations filed briefs in support of the University of Michigan's admissions policy including a prestigious group of retired U.S. military leaders who explained that a racially diverse officer corps, capable of commanding diverse enlisted ranks, is essential to our national security. The briefs collectively urged the Supreme Court to give university officials leeway to choose minorities from the pool of highly qualified applicants. By a 5–4 vote, in June 2003, the Court agreed and upheld the admissions policy at the University of Michigan Law School.

A Message from Garcia

When you work for someone you respect, it is never easy putting your relationship on the line with that person. But true loyalty, like true friendship, is having the personal integrity to remain true to your principles and to your own conscience. While being fiercely loyal is a virtue, it is only a virtue when it is principled.

Despite the complexities of personal and business politics, you should have the courage and conviction of your ideas and be willing to express them, so long as your observations are meant in good faith and without malice. In making a case and advancing your cause, or arguing against one, do not employ gossip or innuendo. It is wrong and will reflect poorly on your own judgment and may impugn your own character more than you might imagine.

If you are the leader of an organization, be sure to encourage all employees to speak openly and honestly about a problem at hand or one that they foresee. Heading off problems before they occur can save you and your company time and money as well as minimize the amount of aggravation that goes into resolving problems. The best leaders encourage debate and are willing to listen to all parties to the discussion.

CHAPTER 39

Successful People Bring Out the Best in Their Team

AT 9:00 IN THE EVENING ON JULY 24, 2002, NINE COAL MINERS were working 240 feet below the surface of the earth in a coal mine near Somerset, Pennsylvania. As they neared the end of their shift, the miners accidentally broke into an adjacent mine that was filled with water. Fifty million gallons of water rushed into the coal mine in which they were working. The miners nearly drowned from the rush of water, but managed to scamper to safety temporarily.

The coal miners faced life-threatening problems while they waited to be rescued. Their air supply may have been contaminated by toxic fumes from the adjacent mine. Hypothermia was possible because of the cold water rushing through the mine. The biggest problem, however, was the 240 feet of earth—the equivalent of a 20-story building—between them and the surface.

Considering all these circumstances, the miners made a decision. They would either survive as a team or die as a team. The men tied themselves together, so the water would not separate them as it continued to rush through the mine.

Above ground, a hastily assembled team crafted a plan to save the men. The first challenge was to make an educated guess about where the miners escaped to when the waters rushed in. The rescuers drilled a six-inch pipe hole into the spot where they hoped the men would be. The guess was correct. When the drill reached the miners, they banged on the pipe to tell the rescue team they were alive. The rescuers pumped heated air through the pipe to control the water level. The warm air also allowed the men to breathe and reduced the risk of hypothermia. The rescuers themselves faced obstacles as they attempted to save the trapped men. The first challenge was getting a drilling rig that would bore a hole through the earth to reach the miners.

Hours later the rig arrived, but shortly after drilling had begun, the 1500-pound diamond-tipped drill bit broke. Incredibly, it would take another 15 hours until drilling could resume. A cap was placed over the rescue shaft so the miners' air pocket would remain pressurized. During the drilling, water was pumped out of the mine, because the miners might drown when the drill pierced the damp cavern where they were trapped. Even after the hole was bored, a dangerous job of raising and lowering the rescue capsule in the 26-inch shaft remained.

While hundreds of rescue workers above the ground were working to overcome the obstacles of reaching them, the miners also did what they could to survive below. They built barricades to channel water away from their air pocket. They huddled together to stay warm and shared the one corn beef sandwich that one of the miners had left in his lunch pail. The men conserved the lights on their hard hats.

Back on the surface Governor Mark Schweiker made sure that the rescuers had whatever equipment they needed to save the men. Along with offering solace, Schweiker kept the families informed of every change in the status of the rescue mission, whether it was positive or negative. His efforts ensured that the families heard every report before the media, and that reporters did not intrude upon anxious family members. The governor threatened to arrest any reporter who attempted to contact the families of the miners during the crisis. Schweiker also helped to coordinate the various agencies involved in the rescue effort.

After an agonizing 77-hour rescue and gut-wrenching set-backs, all nine miners were rescued. The mission was a success because of the teamwork of the miners, as well as the incredible efforts of the rescue workers. All of them did their jobs and never gave up, despite the most adverse of circumstances.

The nine miners kept their hopes up, even though there were many times when it appeared that the rescue mission might have been aborted. With faith, experience, and a little luck, they survived an ordeal that would break most ordinary people. The rescuers displayed creativity and perseverance in accomplishing a mission in which the odds were stacked heavily against them.

Miner Blaine Mayhugh said, "Everyone had strong moments. At any certain time maybe one guy got down, and then the rest pulled together and then that guy would get back up and maybe somebody else would feel a little weaker," Mayhugh said. "But it was a team effort. That's the only way it could've been."[1]

Teamwork Is the Difference Between Success and Failure

Although teamwork usually isn't a life-or-death situation, it often spells the difference between success and failure for the business. A company with many talented employees working separately isn't nearly as successful as one where talented workers work together and believe in the mission. At my company, we work toward common goals and every employee knows the mission.

Colin Powell tells a story about Napoleon Bonaparte. The French general would occasionally mingle with his troops. Bonaparte would ask the lowest-ranking soldier to state the overall mission of the army. Bonaparte believed that if the mission was clear, the soldier would be able to understand and explain it.[2] A successful team knows its mission, whether it's to rescue nine trapped miners or to be the best data mining company in the business. The team leaders must keep the group focused on the mission.

Leaders can also bring out *ganas* in the members of a team. The leader arouses passion and helps put the fire in the members' bellies. As Price Pritchett said, "Once you've pointed people in the right direction, and triggered a powerful internal drive, you need to get the hell out of the way."[3]

Joe Gibbs, the former football coach who now oversees a Winston Cup racing team, knows a great deal about team building. In his book *Racing To Win*, Gibbs discussed the difficulties of building a team when you're motivating people with very different personalities.[4] Some are motivated by praise, whereas others need to be scolded from time to time.

Most of us work harder when we're working as a team. We know others are depending on us and we don't want to let them down. You should feel that same sense of obligation, whether it's a coworker or the members of your family who are depending on you. If you don't feel that sense of obligation to your employer, you need to find another place to work.

Let People Know Their Voices Are Being Heard

Not only do people around you need to buy into your dream, but they also need to have a stake in ownership so as to make the dream their own. This only happens if they have a say in the decision-making process. To unite them toward the same goal, their ideas must be heard, acknowledged, and respected.

Of course, you will not have consensus on every decision, but you must show respect for others' suggestions. Bringing closure to issues that are frequently raised during the course of any business day is essential. People like to know they are heard. Leaders who fail to close the loop frustrate the people who work for them. Maybe it's a boss, who never gets back to you with a response, or perhaps you've applied for a new position in the company and you never got an answer. One day you see someone else working in that position and you never find out why you were turned down.

Closing the loop is a leadership trait you can easily develop. It simply requires discipline and a little backbone. Articulating your reasoning for acting a certain way, taking a certain position, or making a certain decision is not a sign of weakness. On the contrary, it shows you make decisions in a rational way, and helps employees understand why one solution was chosen over another.

Leadership Lessons from Nature

Have you ever looked up to watch a flock of honking geese flying overhead and wondering why they always fly in a V formation? Have you ever thought of these geese as role models? Milton Olson, author of *Lessons from Geese*, makes a compelling case that five behaviors of geese during migration can be translated into leadership lessons for our lives.[5]

1. *First Behavior*: "As each goose flaps its wings, it creates an 'uplift' for the bird following. By flying in a 'V' formation, the whole flock adds 71% greater flying range than if the bird flew alone."

   First Lesson: "People who share a common direction and sense of community can get where they are going quicker and easier because they are traveling on the thrust of one another."

2. *Second Behavior*: "Whenever a goose falls out of formation, it suddenly feels the drag and resistance of trying to fly alone, and quickly gets back into formation to take advantage of the 'lifting power' of the bird immediately in front."

   Second Lesson: "If we have as much sense as a goose, we will stay in formation with those who are headed where we want to go (and be willing to accept their help as well as give ours to the others)."

3. *Third Behavior*: "When the lead goose gets tired, it rotates back into the formation and another goose flies at the point position."

   Third Lesson: "It pays to take turns doing the hard tasks and sharing leadership—with people, as with geese, we are interdependent on each other."

4. *Fourth Behavior*: "The geese in formation honk from behind to encourage those up front to keep up their speed."

   Fourth Lesson: "We need to make sure our honking from behind is encouraging—and not something else."

5. *Fifth Behavior*: "When a goose gets sick or wounded or shot down, two geese drop out of formation and follow it down to help and protect it. They stay with it until it is able to fly again or dies. Then they launch out on their own, with another formation, or catch up with the flock."

   Fifth Lesson: "If we have as much sense as geese, we too will stand by each other in difficult times as well as when we are strong."

A Message from Garcia

Successful people encourage those around them to succeed and are adept at instilling in others a passionate desire for all members to achieve the group's goals. Successful people inspire others to do better each day. The most successful entrepreneurs convince their employees to share in their vision for the company, thus increasing performance and productivity. Some of the ways in which successful leaders accomplish this is by providing ownership or "a stake in the outcome" to members of the team. Listening openly, honestly and intently to suggestions from all individuals and participants who have a stake in the outcome encourages and promotes an environment where all ideas can be advanced, the best of which being employed to achieve the group's goals.

Successful people have great team-building skills. They know they'll go twice as far with a good team surrounding them. The best team players are positive, creative, and have good interpersonal skills. On the other hand, oftentimes cliques form an organization. Cliques are not teams. On the contrary, they often serve to undermine team unity. To remind you of the power of team unity: the next time you hear that all-too-familiar honking and look up at the sky to see geese heading south for the winter while flying in the striking "V" formation, you should remember why they fly that way and the valuable lessons we can learn from them about leadership and teamwork.

PART SIX

SUCCESS STRATEGY 4: PERSEVERE

CHAPTER 40

∙∙

Perseverance Is Everything

THE FINAL STRATEGY IN THE SUCCESS ARSENAL IS TO PERSEVERE. Taking action is important, but perseverance and determination are essential to overcome the challenges and obstacles you face. Just as rejection is only a bump on the road to acceptance, a "no" is just an annoyance on the path to "yes."

In the early part of the twentieth century, with the intention of making one of the world's greatest expeditions, the goal of one man and his crew turned instead into one of mankind's greatest tales of survival. The movie *Shackleton: The Story of Endurance*, tells the fascinating story of Ernest Shackleton, who led a group of adventurers to safety after a trip to Antarctica went awry in 1914. A previous expedition had reached the South Pole, but merely turned around and took the same route back. Sir Ernest Shackleton's goal was to reach the South Pole and then continue on across Antarctica.

Shackleton advertised for men to join him on his expedition. Even though all knew that danger awaited them, 5,000 volunteered. Twenty-seven men were chosen to join him for the journey. In 1914, they left on their great adventure, intending to be the first to reach the South Pole. Ultimately, they failed but their struggle to survive is now a legendary tale about the importance of perseverance.

The story actually begins in 1907 when Shackleton set forth on what was called the Nimrod expedition. During two years, Shackleton and his crew walked and pulled sleds for more than 700 miles before being forced to turn back almost in sight of their goal, less than 100 miles away. To continue would have meant death. Shackleton reasoned that the lead party would not be able to return to their base camp for the safety of all concerned, he chose instead to return.

However, Shackleton was not through. He did not give up. He took a break to regroup and then set out again in 1914 with 27 men on his Imperial Trans-Antarctic expedition aboard the *Endurance*. The ship set sail from the tiny island of Georgia at the bottom of the Atlantic Ocean. Two years later, no one heard from Shackleton and he and his team were presumed dead. In fact, they had survived under the most challenging circumstances imaginable. In sight of their destination, just 97 miles from the South Pole, the *Endurance* became trapped in an ice floe, caught in the Antarctic icepack below Cape Horn.

The men fought to survive yet still pursued their goal of crossing Antarctica. Talk about determination and perseverance! The slogan they lived by was, "By endurance we conquer."[1]

After 11 months of being wedged between glacial icepacks, the boat was eventually crushed. After surviving twenty months living on drifting ice floes on an uninhabited, barren and freezing sub-Antarctic island, Shackleton and five other men then made one of the most harrowing open boat voyages in history. They miraculously landed on the mountainous, glacier-covered island of South Georgia. After four attempts, Shackleton was able to break through the Antarctic ice pack to rescue half of his men. He still did not quit and then went to the rescue the other half of the expedition on the other side of the frozen continent. Shackleton left none of his men behind, and everyone survived.

In comparison to the hardships suffered by Shackleton and his crew, what we might endure to achieve our goals is minimal. I believe virtually any goal can be reached through perseverance. Calvin Coolidge said, "Nothing in the world can take the place of persistence. Talent will not; nothing in the world is more common than unsuccessful men with great talent. Genius will not; unrewarded genius is almost a proverb. Education will not; the world is full of educated derelicts. Persistence and determination alone are omnipotent."[2]

Lincoln Did Not Let Failure Deter Him

Abraham Lincoln became one of our greatest presidents, but on his road to success he faced more obstacles than most of us could possibly imagine. In 1831, his business failed. In 1832, Lincoln was defeated in his bid for the Legislature. In 1833, he failed again in business, and he suffered a nervous breakdown in 1836. Lincoln lost Congressional elections in 1843 and 1848, as well as losses in bids for the Senate and the vice-presidency. After being elected as President in 1860, Lincoln encountered more setbacks. The nation fell apart and the Civil War began.

James Carville and Paul Begala point out that Lincoln was not much of a commander-in-chief at first. In their book, *Buck Up, Suck Up . . . And Come Back When You Foul Up,*[3] they point out that Lincoln lost battles at Manassas, Big Bethel, Kessler's Cross Lanes, Blackburn's Ford, Ball's Bluff, McDowell, Front Royal, Winchester, Cross Keys, Port Republic, Drewry's Bluff, Gaine's Mill, Cedar Mountain, Bristoe State, Thoroughfare Gap, Harper's Ferry, Shepardstown, and the first battle of Fredericksburg. And that was just in the first two years of the war. While he was in office, Lincoln's son, Willie, died. His wife was attacked for being a spendthrift after buying the famous bed in what is now known as the Lincoln bedroom.[4]

Before they became involved in Bill Clinton's campaign, Carville and Begala were quite unsuccessful as political advisors. Carville's candidates couldn't win in Louisiana. The Senate candidate he was advising in Virginia lost the election. And when Carville and Begala teamed up for the first time in Texas, their candidate suffered what was then the worst whipping of a Democrat in Texas history.[5]

Another potential political player put his perspective on the situation. Despite being ridiculed as Ross Perot's running mate, Admiral Stockdale remained courageous and upbeat. He stressed the importance of having the emotional stability to handle failure. You don't have to like to lose, but it shouldn't paralyze you either. You shouldn't be driven to lash out at others or rationalize your failure. Stockdale kept failure in perspective by thinking about men and women like Lincoln who successfully lived with failure in the past.

I do not accept the concept of failure. However, I believe that the only time you truly fail is when you don't learn a lesson. I've been knocked off, of course, but I eventually get to my destination or discover something equally worthwhile along the way.

A Message from Garcia

Only those who have the courage and fortitude to stick to their convictions and pursue their dreams regardless of any and all obstacles, willing to pay any price, will ultimately prevail. This is perhaps the most fundamental character trait in an individual who has achieved extraordinary success in a particular field.

Yes, having a good idea, a plan, and taking action to move toward the goal every day or week is imperative. But having the emotional stamina to withstand the greatest of forces that will invariably challenge you as you move toward the accomplishment of your dream, which may take years, is known as perseverance. Only those with abundant supplies of it are destined for ultimate victory. The brass ring only goes to those who sweat and struggle and work and who never quit, who believe in themselves and the goal of their organization.

This means doing whatever it takes for as long as possible. Period. Perseverance means you hit a roadblock and you go around it or drive through it. Perseverance means you come upon some challenge and use all your resources and creative energy to find an alternate route. To an individual with perseverance, the words *no* and *never* mean nothing. Phrases such as "it can't be done" and "it's crazy" mean simply that no one has ever done it before. You can and you will.

CHAPTER 41

Don't Be Afraid to Get Your Hands Dirty

THE MOST SUCCESSFUL PEOPLE DON'T VIEW THEMSELVES AS BEING better than anyone else. They are willing to lend a hand, contribute and pitch in wherever help is necessary. Bill Crawford, our janitor at the Academy, was a walking example of someone who didn't view hard work as beneath him. Until one cadet stumbled upon his war record, no one knew he had won the Medal of Honor. Here was a Medal of Honor winner willing to clean toilets and scrub floors.

Some CEOs remain aloof and may even have a separate bathroom in their office. Employees quickly become wise to the CEO who talks the talk but doesn't walk the walk. They know that this is someone who will send them into battle, but won't lead them there.

Herb Kelleher turned Southwest Airlines into one of the most admired companies in the country by creating a culture where employees, whether they were pilots or ramp agents, pitched in to get the job done. When mechanics on the graveyard shift complained that their hours kept them from participating in company picnics and barbecues, Kelleher held separate events for them at 2:00 in the morning and he showed up as the chef.[1]

The successful PBS television series *Back to the Floor* asks CEOs to spend a week doing the work of low-level employees. The series is a big hit in the United Kingdom and a U.S. version was created.

CEOs agreed to spend time working at some of the toughest jobs in their company. The executives featured on the program were required to work the full shift, handling all of the grueling duties of the position.

Bob Dickinson, president of Carnival Cruise Lines, spent a week on one of his ships handling a variety of jobs. Dickinson served drinks on deck in the blazing sun. He cleaned rooms. He even entertained at one of the shows. He was reprimanded for being late for one of his jobs, and saw for himself how tough many positions are.[2] Spending time outside the executive suite is an eye-opener for a leader and is, most of all, a way for the leader to create relationships based on mutual respect and appreciation.

Remember, while you might be a good CEO, it's unlikely you'll excel at all the jobs at your company. A field experience like this shows you how important those jobs are for your company's success. You also will realize how difficult they can be.

A Message from Garcia
....

Successful people genuinely believe that they're no better than anyone in their organization. They're willing to pitch in wherever they are needed. By taking time to work side by side with employees, executives can inspire and motivate them. The best executives make it their business to get to know firsthand what their employees do and how they do it. This can be tremendously inspiring to the CEO.

Only in this way can employees see that the CEO is someone who strives to understand all facets of the business and that the CEO understands their needs and concerns when making a decision. Most importantly, employees feel that the CEO who takes the time to understand them is someone for whom they will put in the extra effort. Furthermore, CEOs who exercise this type of management style are likely to come upon a new idea, technique or method by working firsthand on the jobs that need to be done, thus coming up with new and innovative ways to enhance productivity and profitability. CEOs who operate this way are likely to win the hearts and minds of their employees, which translates to better employee morale, increased business, and more efficiency.

CHAPTER 42

....

Work Hard, Surf Hard

WHEN BILL BENNETT WAS THE DRUG CZAR, A POLITICAL APPOINTEE with as high a media profile as is possible, he shunned the Washington social scene in favor of a more reserved personal life. But it wasn't all work and no play for Bennett. Most Sundays a group of us would play a spirited game of touch football with Bennett. In fact, when I first interviewed with Bennett as a White House Fellow, he first asked me if I was any good at football.

Bennett looked at sports as a metaphor for life and he believed that sports are a way to learn, after either victory or defeat, that another day, another chance, comes tomorrow. And sports are a good way to put work behind you for a little while.[1]

Sports and activities have always been a big part of my life. When growing up in Panama, I used to ride horses competitively. One of my favorite activities at the Air Force Academy was soaring. A plane pulls your glider off the ground until you reach 10,000 feet. You pull the cord and your glider is released. You soar through the air, looking for the lift that will take you higher and higher. Your glider stays aloft until you can no longer find the lift and you land. While at the Academy, I also enjoyed freefall parachuting, and in my younger days I spent a lot of time scuba diving. Just as football put some distance between Bennett and the office, so surfing renews my energy. I also enjoy riding my Harley Davidson motorcycle that I take on the back roads or throttle along the ocean route on A1A from Boca Raton to Palm Beach.

One thing I do that doesn't increase my insurance rates is playing bridge. Playing bridge well requires a great deal of strategy and forces you to use your math skills.

There are other activities that can help improve reasoning, thinking ability, and analytic skills. Chess is probably one of the best. The New York–based Chess-in-the-Schools program is a non-profit organization that sends chess instructors into poor neighborhoods to help kids learn the game.

Chess is an inexpensive way to empower and inspire kids to succeed. Players learn how to think logically, and playing chess can have a positive impact on academic performance. At Miami Jackson Senior High School, Mario Martinez coached the chess team to eight county championships, five state championships, and five national titles. He says, "Chess teaches us that choices have consequences."[2]

Bring Balance to Your Life

Achieving success is about being able to achieve balance in your life between work, play, and family. The elder George Bush put work and family in perspective. He said, "Now that my political days are over, I can honestly say that the three most rewarding titles I've held are the only three I have left—a husband, a father, and a granddad."[3]

The best situation to be in is to have a job you love and to be surrounded by good people with whom you enjoy working. It's never worth working at a job you hate, even if the money is great. Even if you enjoy your work immensely, you should take time out for real relaxation and time with your family and friends and involvement in a sport or hobby that takes your mind off work. Colin Powell believes this. He advised a group of newly appointed ambassadors to take their jobs seriously but still have fun. In his first major speech to personnel in the State Department, Powell told them to do their work and go home to their families.[4]

A Message from Garcia

While some successful people do nothing but work, the happiest successful people are those who manage to have balance in their lives. This means finding time for your family and friends. This means finding time to unwind through some sport, hobby, or other activity that gets your mind off your work. This is healthy. This is not only good for your mind and your body—it can even have rewards for your business.

It is important to be able to get away from the office. By doing so, it can give you a new, refreshed, and invigorated perspective when not mentally dwelling on a problem or situation. Stepping back can help you see things that you might not be able to see when you are close to something all of the time. Even if you're a type-A personality, you need to take a break from work. You'll find that these interludes clear your head and allow you to be more creative. Keeping all aspects of your life in balance will prevent potential breakdowns, especially in difficult times. Take a hike, play with your kids, and take a moment to appreciate your life. Stay in touch with those who love you and those whom you love.

CHAPTER 43

··

Respond to and Learn from Adversity

BREE WALKER WAS A SUCCESSFUL ANCHORWOMAN FOR MANY YEARS in Southern California and is now married to Jim Lampley, the NBC and HBO broadcaster. The parents of two children, she and Lampley live in Utah, where they own a very successful restaurant, as well as a production company. In her spare time, Walker loves to jump horses. Walker suffers from ectrodactyly, a genetic abnormality of the hands or feet. To ride, she uses special reins and horse tack that she helped design. Along with her professional accomplishments, she is a nationally known advocate for the disabled and has helped many people with disabilities enter professions in the media.

Adversity comes in different forms. You need mental toughness and resiliency to overcome it. When Tom Cruise first came to Hollywood, he auditioned for a role. Cruise was told that he wasn't good-looking enough to be an actor and should concentrate on getting a tan during his brief stay in Hollywood.[1] Cruise certainly proved the auditioner wrong.

We often look at successful people and don't realize how much adversity they encountered on their way to their success. Mel Gibson's childhood wasn't easy. He grew up in poverty in Peekskill, New York. He was one of 11 children. His father worked as a railroad brakeman until he sustained severe injuries in a job-related accident. The accident forced the Gibson family to rely on public assistance. Gibson lacked direction as a young adult and held many menial jobs such as bagging groceries and waxing surfboards. He finally discovered his passion when his sister filled out an application on his behalf for drama school.[2]

Most successful people have paid their dues and didn't have an easy road to success. Diana Krall is a very successful jazz musician who won her first Grammy in 2002. When her album hit the top of the jazz album charts, Krall was viewed by some as an overnight success. Those observers didn't realize that she was 37 years old and had been a professional musician for 15 years. Krall didn't record her first album until age 28 and really didn't achieve any recognition until she was in her thirties.[3]

For every Krall who finds success after years of adversity, there are thousands of musicians who never make it. Every day, these musicians have people telling them they'll never make it in show business. Rejection is a way of life. The ones who do make it, however, are those who have found a way to overcome adversity.

Adversity Makes You Tougher, Stronger, and More Resolved

Author Paul Stolz believes that adversity is one of the best teachers there is. Stolz defines adversity quotient (AQ) as the measure of one's ability to handle adversity.[4] Adversity should make you stronger, tougher, and more resolute. It should heighten your desire to succeed, not diminish it. Take the hand you're dealt and play it as best you can. The satisfaction that comes from overcoming adversity makes success that much sweeter.

Charles Schwab, head of the giant financial services firm, and Richard Branson, founder of Virgin Airlines, succeeded in spite of dyslexia. Thousands of other entrepreneurs, CEOs, business leaders, writers, performers, scientists, and inventors have also succeeded in spite of having dyslexia or another form of learning disability. There are even scholars who believe that Albert Einstein suffered from dyslexia.

Einstein, depending on which report you read, did not begin speaking until he was at least 3 years old. The legendary scientist did not learn how to tie his shoes until he was at least 9 and some believe he never mastered this talent. His teachers had few good words to say about him. Despite these problems, Einstein, of course, is recognized as one of the most brilliant people who ever lived.

When you face adversity, the road to success is most assuredly harder, but it is not impassable. Although you may have limitations, you undoubtedly have strengths. You need to focus on those strengths and use them to pursue your passion, no matter how much adversity may lie in your path.

A Message from Garcia

Someone once said, "whatever does not kill us makes us stronger." Life is filled with moments and challenges that will truly test us. These may be physical liabilities that you possess from birth or setbacks that you have endured during your life. Adversity is just another word for challenge and all adversity must be met and overcome in order for you to succeed. Some of the most successful people have started on their journeys to fame and fortune from points of despair and depression. The difference is that they don't use the argument that life is unfair to prevent them from going after what they want. They get over their fears and they succeed in spite of the cards they have been dealt.

Giving up in response to adversity is an admission that you're not finding solutions to your problems. In their personal lives everyone has adversity to overcome. The family unit becomes even stronger each time it overcomes adversity together. During difficult periods, family members can point to those tough times and take comfort from their triumphs. After every setback, jot down a list of lessons learned and think carefully about your next move. Note what you think are the key reasons for what went wrong and how you might address those problems if you were to face them again.

Believe in Yourself
and Stand by
Your Convictions

ONE OF THE REASONS I WENT TO THE AIR FORCE ACADEMY WAS TO be independent of my father. By getting into the Academy, which I was able to do through scholarships, I didn't have to rely on my father to help pay my tuition. If my father paid my tuition, I would have to answer to my dad, "El Tigre," about my grades and I did not want that. My desire to attend the Air Force Academy was also fueled by the challenge of succeeding at a school that is one of the toughest in the United States.

Obtaining recommendations for my application to the Air Force Academy was an important part of the process. I asked my high school principal for one, and he told me that he couldn't recommend me because I wasn't involved in Junior ROTC; I'd be taking away a spot at a service academy from someone who was more deserving.

To get that recommendation, I went from shooting spitballs at the Junior ROTC cadets to being one of those guys parading around in boots and uniform, having spitballs shot at me, and bearing the brunt of the mocking of my friends. Much to my surprise however, not only did I like Junior ROTC, but I also discovered that I was good at it. I ended up joining the elite Rangers program. The challenge of doing well in that program excited me and pushed me forward. After two years of Junior ROTC, I finally earned the recommendation from my principal.

As I progressed through Junior ROTC and the Air Force Academy, I enjoyed learning about leadership and honor. I was proud of my military service. I doubt I would have made it through the Academy just to prove a point to my father. Even though I didn't know it at the time, it appears as though I was pursuing my passion.

Although my father wasn't happy with me being in the military, he put a lot of weight and credence in character traits such as discipline, honor, and integrity. There was no better place on earth than the Air Force Academy to build those traits.

Years later, my father came to respect my decision to join the military. Family members were invited to a ceremony at the White House for White House Fellows and got to meet President Reagan. Because of my father's keen interest in American government and history, he was as excited as I was to be there. My father knew I would never have been a White House Fellow if I hadn't gone to the Air Force Academy and joined the military.

Through all of my successes and setbacks, I believed in myself. Could I have taken an easier path? Yes. Did I have to fight my father and work incredibly hard to gain admission to the U.S. Air Force Academy? Did I have total faith in my ability to achieve this goal? Absolutely. Would I have gone as far without believing in myself and without a burning desire to succeed? Absolutely not.

Standing by Your Convictions Pays Off

Actress and screenwriter Nia Vardalos isn't the prettiest woman in Hollywood, but she certainly is someone who believes in herself. She wrote the screenplay for the hit movie *My Big Fat Greek Wedding*. She also stars in the movie, but that wasn't necessarily going to be the case if Vardalos had left her fate in others' hands. Vardalos refused to sell her screenplay to those interested in making it unless she was allowed to star in it. She believed in herself as an actress and was willing to risk losing a short-term windfall so she could achieve her long-term goal.

As a firm, Sterling Financial stands by its convictions. We are one of a handful of investment banking/research companies that has the courage to make "sell" recommendations in the face of tremendous pressure to do otherwise. As you might imagine, companies would like us to report only good news. In fact, we report our findings whether they are good or bad, regardless of the consequences. Because of Sterling Financial's reputation for excellent, unbiased research, a negative report from us often causes a company's stock to drop. As you might also imagine, this doesn't make us the most popular firm on Wall Street.

A Message from Garcia

Success is about pursuing your passions, not someone else's dreams. Although your parents may want you to pursue a safe and traditional path to achieve their version of success, it may not be the one that's right for you. And if you're a parent, remember that if you have done your job well, the best you can hope for is that your children are happy with whatever it is they do in life—regardless of their job or who they marry. Success is not necessarily measured by someone's bank account, but by the depth of their soul and the contribution they make to others.

Let parents and mentors guide you. Consider their advice carefully because they truly care for you. If you are a child you must respect your parents and understand that they are only offering you advice that is meant to help you. You may not see that now, but sometimes it takes years to accept that. However, whether you are an adult or a child, the fact is that no matter how hard you work, it's virtually impossible to reach success in a field that you really dislike. Once you have identified your passion and your strengths in life, let them guide you on your road to success. Remember, success is not about money; it's about finding your calling in life and pursuing it regardless of financial gain.

CHAPTER 45

....

A Final Message
from Garcia

RONALD REAGAN'S PHILOSOPHY OF LIFE WAS SIMPLE BUT POIGNANT. According to Edmund Morris, the former president's official biographer, Reagan believed in these simple truths: that prayers are answered; that the common man is wise; and that life with a woman who loves you is the closest thing to heaven you can find.[1]

What principles guide you from day to day? Write them down and examine whether they're negative or positive. Look inwardly to see if you've become jaded and cynical. Do your views reflect that the world is a good or bad place? Is your life filled with happiness or unpleasant experiences?

How do the principles you live by compare with the success beliefs we discussed? Do you have a passion for succeeding? Do you show the initiative of a Lieutenant Rowan? Do you treat everyone you meet with respect and try to learn from them? Are honor, integrity, loyalty, and veracity important to you? Do you love to learn and learn from your mistakes? Do you give back to the community?

If your approach to life has left you unhappy, and unsuccessful, maybe it's time for a fresh start. If you feel your life has little meaning, do something of substance today to make it more meaningful.

Develop a Philosophy of Life

Like any business plan, your life plan should be constantly reevaluated. If you're at point A, you constantly should ask yourself how you can get to point B. If you're stuck, your mentor can help. If you don't have a mentor who can help, research strategies for getting from point A to point B. Look for books by people who've achieved the kind of success you're seeking. You have to map out your plan for getting from point A to point B.

Even if you think you don't have the time to follow through on your plan, you're wrong. Even if you only "waste" one hour per day online or watching television, that's about 30 hours per month that you could devote to the pursuit of your dreams.

Financial planners often recommend that you track how much you spend in the course of a day or week. Start tracking how much time you're losing over the course of a day or week. If you use that wasted time to focus on your goals, you'll be on the fast track to success.

Like any good distance runner, you need to learn how to pace yourself over the long haul, but you also need an extra spurt of energy as the finish line comes into view. If you run out of energy during any of these stages of your journey, you'll never reach your goals.

How Do You Measure Success?

Define what success means to you. Hopefully it's not just money. In the movie, *Wall Street*, Martin Sheen argues with his son, Charlie Sheen, over whether Michael Douglas intends to exploit the father's company, which is the subject of a takeover bid. The father said to his son, "What you see is a man who never measured a man's success by the size of his wallet." How do you measure success? Does success mean providing for your family and raising good kids? Are there people in your life who love you and believe in you? What gives you a sense of satisfaction? Ask yourself how you want to be remembered. If you wrote your own eulogy today, what would it say? What would you like it to say?

Ralph Waldo Emerson defined success with these words: "To laugh often and much; to win the respect of intelligent people and the affection of children; to earn the appreciation of honest critics and endure the betrayal of false friends; to appreciate beauty; to find the best in others; to leave the world a bit better; and whether by a healthy child, a garden patch or a redeemed social condition; to know even one life has breathed easier because you lived. This is to have succeeded."[2]

Former President George Bush said, in his 1989 inaugural address, "We are not the sum of our possessions. They are not the measure of our lives. In our hearts we know what matters. We cannot hope only to leave our children a bigger car, a bigger bank account. We must hope to give them a sense of what it means to be a loyal friend; a loving parent; a citizen who leaves his home, his neighborhood, and his town better than he found it."[3]

With the Right Life Philosophy, You Can Succeed

- I wouldn't have written this book if I didn't believe it would help people succeed. I believe we get the success that we deserve. If we work hard at it and are willing to learn and change, we will succeed.
- My philosophy of life is that the good guys always win. If you commit yourself to values like integrity and honor, you'll always come out ahead.
- I believe everything happens for a reason and there are no coincidences. If you assume everyone has something to teach you, there are no chance encounters because you'll learn from each and every person you meet.

- I believe strongly in pursuing your passions in whatever field makes you happy. You can pursue those passions by finding a mentor who's already established in the field that intrigues you and follow their advice closely.
- Write down your dreams using the Success Compass™ and carry it with you all the time or request an email reminder. Refer to it often and focus on what it is you want to achieve. Make sure you're making progress toward your goals every day.
- Take the word failure out of your vocabulary. Learn from every mistake you make and try again with the knowledge you gained.
- You should always pursue excellence, both in business and personally. Every day, you should make a conscious effort to do better as a human being.
- Public service is the responsibility of all of us, and we owe a duty to the community we live in.
- Finally, I believe that each of us has *ganas*, the desire to achieve more. With *ganas* you can achieve your dreams. If you don't have it now, you need to find what puts a fire in your belly.

What is the legacy that you hope to leave behind? If it's only money and material things, it won't be much of a legacy. Grab hold of your own torch and charge forward, shedding light toward a future that is bright and filled with opportunity.

Endnotes

Chapter 3

1. Buckingham, Marcus, and Clifton, Donald O., *Now, Discover Your Strengths*, NY, FreePress, 2001.

Chapter 4

1. Anonymous, *It Works*, Marina Del Rey, CA, De Vorss Publications, 1926.
2. Kelman, Charles D. *Through My Eyes: The Story of a Surgeon Who Dared to Take on the Medical World*, NY, Crown Publishers, 1985.

Chapter 5

1. Hubbard, Elbert, *A Message to Garcia*, NY, Peter Pauper Press (1983).
2. Tracy, Brian, *Focal Point*, New York, Amacom, 2002, p. 77.
3. Hargrove, Robert, *E-Leader: Reinventing Leadership in a Connected Economy*, Cambridge, Perseus Publishing, 2001, p. 20.
4. *Investor's Business Daily*, October 1, 2001, p. A4.

Chapter 6

1. Maxwell, John, *The 21 Irrefutable Laws of Leadership*, Nashville, TN, Thomas Nelson, 1998, pp. 168–178.
2. *Investor's Business Daily*, September 6, 2001, p. A4.
3. Finley, Anita, "Clark, The Oldest Man to Circle the Planet Alone Under Sail," *Boomer Times & Senior Life*, March 2002, p. 45.
4. See www.vincelombardi.com/quotes/desire.htm.

Chapter 7

1. "Preacher, Teacher, Gadfly," *Time*, July 18, 1988, p. 58.
2. Matthews, Jay, *Escalante: The Best Teacher in America*, New York, Henry Holt, 1988, p. 291.

3. Garcia, Charles Patrick, "The Knock and Announce Rule: A New Approach to the Destruction-of-Evidence Exception," *Columbia Law Review*, Volume 93, 1993, p. 685.

Chapter 8

1. *Investor's Business Daily*, August 23, 2001, p. A3.

Chapter 9

1. Rebbe Nachman of Breslov, *The Empty Chair: Finding Hope and Joy*, Jewish Lights Publishing, 1994, p. 113.
2. Thomas, Marlo, *The Right Words at the Right Time*, New York, Atria Books, 2002, p. 232.
3. Thomas, p. 234.
4. *Investor's Business Daily*, May 20, 2001, p. A4.
5. *Checkpoints*, Spring 2002, p. 40.
6. Collins, Jim, *Good to Great: Why Some Companies Make the Leap... and Others Don't*, New York, HarperCollins, 2001, p. 85.
7. Harari, Oren, *The Leadership Secrets of Colin Powell*, New York, McGraw-Hill Trade, 2002, pp. 215–216.
8. "Perfect Game Shocks Ailing Vero Man," *South Florida Sun-Sentinel*, July 20, 2002, p. 2-C.

Chapter 10

1. Text of the speech is reproduced from Department of Defense Pamphlet GEN-1A, U.S. Government Printing Office, 1964.
2. Krzyzewski, Mike, and Phillips, Donald T., *Coaching with the Heart: Coach K's Successful Strategies for Basketball, Business and Life*, New York, Warner Books, 2000, p. 47.
3. Gormley, Michael, "Merrill Lynch to Pay $100M in Penalties," *South Florida Sun-Sentinel*, May 22, 2002, p. 1-D.
4. *Investor's Business Daily*, September 24, 2001, p. A4.
5. Pitino, Rick, *Lead to Succeed*, New York, Broadway Books, 2000, p. 74.
6. Cohen, William A., *The New Art of the Leader: Leading with Integrity and Honor*, Paramus, NJ, Prentice Hall, 2000, p. 170.
7. "Ann Landers," *South Florida Sun-Sentinel*, April 27, 2002, p. 2-D.

Chapter 12

1. Miller, William Lee, "Thinking Like Lincoln," *Bottom Line Personal*, July 1, 2002, p. 9.

2. Miller, p. 9.
3. Miller, p. 9.
4. *Investor's Business Daily*, September 14, 2001, p. A4.
5. Kotter, John P., *Leading Change*, Boston, Harvard Business School Press, 1996, p. 175.
6. Kotter, p. 178.
7. Foundation for Enterprise Development, www.fed.org.
8. Kotter, pp. 183–184.
9. *My Generation*, July-August 2002, p. 58.
10. *Investor's Business Daily*, June 1, 2001, p. A4.

Chapter 13

1. Carpenter, Susan, and Farlie, Maggie, "Solo Adventurer Circles the World," *South Florida Sun-Sentinel*, July 3, 2002, p. 1-A.
2. Maxwell, John C., *Failing Forward: Turning Mistakes Into Stepping Stones*, Thomas Nelson, 2000, p. 2.
3. Mayer, Jeffrey J., *Success Is a Journey: 7 Steps to Achieving Success in the Business Life*, New York, McGraw-Hill, 1999, pp. 16–17.
4. Maxwell, p. 17.

Chapter 14

1. *My Generation*, July-August 2002, p. 58.
2. "Spread the Inspiration," *USA Weekend*, April 19–21, 2002, p. 4.
3. Wilson, Pat, "Bosemer Hosts Caring Hearts Awards," *Boca Raton Times*, April 17, 2002, p. 17.
4. Herman, Tom, "Ask Dow Jones," *South Florida Sun-Sentinel*, April 28, 2002, p. B7.
5. Kennedy, Caroline, "The Courage Within," *USA Weekend*, June 7–9, 2002, p. 6.

Chapter 15

1. *The Spear Report*, vol. 8m, no. 18, May 6, 2002, p. 1.
2. Harari, Oren, *The Leadership Secrets of Colin Powell*, New York, McGraw-Hill Trade, 2002, pp. 20–21.
3. Edwards, Paul and Sarah, "Three Tips for Making Your Small Business Bigger," *The Costco Connection*, June 2002, p. 13.
4. Chopra, Deepak, "SynchroDestiny," *Miracle Journeys Magazine*, May/June 2002, p. 28.
5. Chopra, p. 29.

Chapter 16

1. Graham, Stedman, *You Can Make It Happen*, New York, Simon & Schuster, 1997, p. 51.
2. Kanchier, Carole, "Does Your Attitude Limit Your Options?" *USA Weekend*, April 12–14, 2002, p. B6.
3. Stroder, Mark E., "Life Coach," *The Costco Connection*, April 2002, pp. 20, 22.
4. Koch, Neil, "I Lost It at the Movies," *Inc.*, May 2002, p. 48.
5. Hill, Napolean, *Think and Grow Rich*, New York, Fawcett Books, 1990, p. 12.
6. *Investor's Business Daily*, September 20, 2001, p. A4.
7. *Investor's Business Daily*, March 7, 2001, p. A4.
8. Krzyzewski, Mike, and Phillips, Donald T., *Coaching with the Heart: Coach K's Successful Strategies for Basketball, Business and Life*, New York, Warner Books, 2000, p. 282.

Chapter 17

1. Brady, Shelly, "Success Secrets from Ace Salesman Bill Porters," *Bottom Line Personal*, August 1, 2002, p. 9.
2. McCarthy, Dennis, "What Obstacles?: This Gutsy Kid Will Stop at Nothing to Become a Doctor," *The Daily News of Los Angeles*, May 19, 2002, p. N1.
3. Kelly, Omar, "Miami Walk-On Outruns Obstacles," *South Florida Sun-Sentinel*, May 13, 2002, p. 1-C.
4. Fittipaldo, Ray, "Not Just for Kicks," *Pittsburgh Post-Gazette*, July 25, 2002, p. 1-D.

Chapter 20

1. Mayer, Jeffrey J., *Success Is a Journey: 7 Steps to Achieving Success in the Business of Life*, New York, McGraw-Hill, 1999, pp. 96–97.

Chapter 21

1. "Thor Heyerdahl, Adventurer Who Sailed on 'Kon-Tiki' Raft," *South Florida Sun-Sentinel*, April 19, 2002, p. 7B, www.trussel.com.
2. Hill, Napoleon, *Napoleon Hill's Keys to Success: The 17 Principles of Personal Achievement*, New York, Plume, 1987, p. 26.
3. Lambert, Bruce, "That's The 'New Spirit,'" *South Florida Sun-Sentinel*, May 2, 2002, p. 3-A.
4. Stockdale, Jim and Sybil, *In Love & War*, New York, Harper & Row, 1984, cover jacket, p. 101.

5. Collins, Jim, *Good to Great: Why Some Companies Make the Leap ... and Others Don't*, New York, HarperCollins, 2001, p. 84.
6. Collins, p. 84.

Chapter 22

1. The article appears in the Sept./Oct. 1997 issue of *Technique*, Vol. 17, No. 9. (reproduced on this website) Elko, Kevin, "The Ultimate Secrets of Goal Setting," www.usa-gymnastics.org/publications.
2. Braun, Chip, "Trophy Hunt Stardom Promises Many Rewards for Ricky Williams," *The Dallas Morning News*, Dec. 10, 1998, p. 1B.

Chapter 23

1. Weil, Martin, "Benjamin O. Davis Jr., 89, Leading Air Force General," *South Florida Sun-Sentinel*, July 7, 2002, p. 6-B.

Chapter 24

1. "Street, 61, Helps Barry Earn Berth in NCAA Championship," *South Florida Sun-Sentinel*, May 7, 2002, p. 2c.
2. CNNSI.com—Golf Plus, December 10, 2001.
3. Mabe, Chauncey, "Prolific Writer Penned Nancy Drew," *South Florida Sun-Sentinel*, May 20, 2002, p. 1-A.
4. Emily Toth, "Are You Old or Are You Sage," *Chronicle of Higher Education*, July 20, 2001, p. 24.
5. Ishoy, Ron, "Soldier of Healing: Retired General Plans to Aid Poor as Medical Missionary," *The Miami Herald*, May 4, 1997, Sunday Broward Edition, p. 1B.
6. Henderson, Carter, *I Don't Feel Old: How to Flourish After 50*, Oakland, CA, Institute for Contemporary Studies, 2002, p. 25.

Chapter 25

1. Ryan, Michael, "An American Success Story," *Parade*, June 30, 2002, p. 4.
2. Moritz, Owen, "Committee Picks Book to Bind City," *New York Daily News*, May 9, 2002, p. 10.
3. Hudson, Mike, "Author James McBride Tells His Mother's Story," *The Roanoke Times & World News*, November 19, 1997, p. 1.

Chapter 26

1. Hargrove, Robert, *E-Leader: Reinventing Leadership in a Connected Economy*, Cambridge, Perseus Publishing, 2001, p. 36.

2. Garreau, Joel, "Frisbee's Spinsmeister; Ed Headrick, The Hero of Circles,"*The Washington Post*, August 15, 2002, p. C1.
3. Ancona, Paula, *Successabilities!* Indianapolis, IN, Jist, 1998, p. 118.
4. Hill, Napoleon, *Napoleon Hill's Keys to Success: The 17 Principles of Personal Achievement*, New York, Dutton, 1994, p. 215.
5. Tracy, Brian, *Focal Point*, New York, Amacom, 2002, p. 190–191.

Chapter 27

1. Endlich, Lisa, *Goldman Sachs: The Culture of Success*, New York, Alfred Knopf, 1999, pp. 88–89.
2. Endlich, p. 17.
3. Endlich, pp. 12, 18.
4. Russell, Joel, "2002 Hispanic Business Fastest-Growing 100," *Hispanic Business*, July/August 2002, p. 36.
5. Axelrod, Alan, *Patton on Leadership*, Paramus, NJ, Prentice Hall, 1999, p. 126.
6. Rosner, Bob, "A Couple of Minutes with Ken Blanchard," workoplis.com, March 1, 2001.
7. Hill, Napoleon, *Napoleon Hill's Keys to Success: The 17 Principles of Personal Achievement*, New York, Dutton, 1994, p. 217.
8. Thomas, Marlo, *The Right Words at the Right Time*, New York, Atria Books, 2002, p. 172.

Chapter 28

1. Morris Jim, *The Oldest Rookie: Big League Dreams From A Small-Town Guy,* Little, Brown, & Co., 2001.
2. Ortega, Bob, *The Untold Story of Sam Walton and Wal-Mart, The World's Most Powerful Retailer*; New York, Times Books, 1998, p. 140.
3. Maxwell, John, *The 21 Irrefutable Laws of Leadership*, Nashville, TN, Thomas Nelson, 1998, p. 171.

Chapter 29

1. Quote is anonymous.
2. Stockdale, James B., *A Vietnam Experience*, Stanford, CA, Hoover Institution, p. 141.
3. Morrell, Margot, and Capparell, Stephanie, *Shackleton's Way: Leadership Lessons from the Great Arctic Explorer*, New York, Viking, 2001, p. 75.
4. *Investor's Business Daily*, July 28, 2002, p. A4.
5. Semler, Ricardo, *Maverick*, New York, Warner Books, 1993, p. 173.
6. Harari, Oren, *Leadership Secrets of Colin Powell*, New York, McGraw-Hill, 2002, pp. 179–180.

7. Pritchett, Price, *Carpe Mañana*, Dallas, Pritchett Rummler-Brache, 2000, p. 1.

Chapter 30

1. Williams, Marjorie. "Manager-in-Chief's Preferred Techniques," *The Washington Post*, December 3, 1986, p. A17.
2. Stroder, Mark E., "Life Coach," *The Costco Connection*, March 2002, p. 20.
3. Michael Jordan Fan Site, www.toppics4u.com.
4. Buckingham, Marcus, and Clifton, Donald O., *Now, Discover Your Strengths*; p. 8.
5. NBC Today Show anchors: Matt Lauer & Katie Couric, Interview with Ron Howard, May 9, 2002.

Chapter 31

1. Matthews, Jay, *Escalante: The Best Teacher in America*, New York, Henry Holt, 1988, p. 308.
2. Rochlin, Margy, "'Ya-Ya' Director Bristles at 'Chick Flick' Label," *Palm Beach Post*, June 8, 2002, p. 1-D.
3. www.sacbee.com, www.mcdonalds.com.
4. Thomas, Marlo, *The Right Words At the Right Time*, New York, Atria Books, 2002, p. 9; *Bottom Line Personal*, September 1, 2002.

Chapter 32

1. Bouchette, Ed, "Omar Khan Fills Important Position for the Steelers— Off the Field," *Pittsburgh Post-Gazette*, March 10, 2002, p. B3.
2. Janson, Chris, *You Can Make It Happen*, New York, Simon & Schuster, 1997, p. 80.
3. Janson, p. 81.
4. Krauthammer, Charles, "A Man for All Seasons," *The Washington Post*, Aug. 25, 2000, p. A31.
5. Kanchier, Carole, "Does Your Attitude Limit Your Options?" *USA Weekend*, April 12–14, 2002, p. B6.
6. Farrington, Brendan, "Taking Time to Teach," *South Florida Sun-Sentinel*, April 29, 2002, p. 6-B.
7. Schwager, Jack, *Market Wizards: Interviews with Top Traders*, Harper Business, NY, 1993.
8. Schwartz, Martin, *Pit Bull: Lessons from Wall Street's Champion Trader*, Harper Business, NY, 1999.

Chapter 33

1. *The Bench Press*, vol. 2, no. 7, October 1998; www.crf.usa.org.
2. www.marvacollins.com.
3. Shribman, David M., *I Remember My Teacher: 365 Reminiscences of Teachers Who Changed Our Lives*, Kansas City, MO, Andrews McMeel, 2002, p. 16.
4. Olson, Cheryl K., "How to Raise an Upbeat Child," *Bottom Line Personal*, May 15, 2002, p. 10.
5. "Dear Abby," *South Florida Sun-Sentinel*, April 27, 2002, p. D6.

Chapter 36

1. Cohen, William A., *The New Art of The Leader: Leading with Integrity and Honor,* Paramus, NJ, Prentice Hall, 2000, p. 47–78.
2. See the U.S. Air Force Academy web site at www.usafa.af.mil.
3. Heim, Pat, and Chapman, Elwood, *Learning to Lead*, Menlo Park, CA, Crisp Publications, 1990, p. 17.
4. Hill, Napolean, *Napoleon Hill's Keys to Success: The 17 Principles of Personal Achievement*, New York, Dutton, 1994, pp. 25–28.
5. Sonnenschein, William, *The Diversity Toolkit*, McGraw-Hill NY, 1999, p. 180.
6. *Investor's Business Daily*, May 18, 2001, p. A4.
7. Harari, Oren, *Leadership Secrets of Colin Powell*, New York, McGraw-Hill, 2002, p. 13.
8. Harari, p. 21.
9. Harari, pp. 23–24.
10. *Investor's Business Daily*, May 14, 2001, p. A4.
11. http://www.anonymousoldChineseproverb.pe.ca/montaguehigh/quotes2.htm.

Chapter 37

1. Miller, William Lee, "Thinkin' Like Lincoln," *Bottom Line Personal*, July 1, 2002, p. 9.
2. www.pbs.org/newshour/debatingourdestiny.
3. Humes, James C., "When It's Your Turn to Speak: Lessons from History's Greatest Orators," *Bottom Line Personal*, May 15, 2002, p. 13.
4. *Investor's Business Daily*, July 29, 2002, p. A4.
5. "Stephen King on How to Write," *Bottom Line Personal*, June 1, 2002, p. 12.

Chapter 38

1. *Investor's, Business Daily*, November 16, 2001, p. A4.
2. Morrell, Margot, and Capparell, Stephanie, *Shackleton's Way: Leadership Lessons from the Great Arctic Explorer*, New York, Viking, 2001, p. 9.

3. Morrell and Capparell, p. 10.
4. Commisso, Marco, "Charles in Charge," *Boca Raton News*, June 4, 2000, p. 1.
5. Freedman, David H., *Corps Business: The 30 Management Principles of the U.S. Marines*, New York, Harper Business, 2000, p. 79.

Chapter 39

1. (editorial) "Making a Miracle," *The Daily News of Los Angeles*, July 30, 2002, p. N12.
2. Harari, Oren, "Lessons from Colin Powell on How to Be a Successful Leader," *Bottom Line Personal*, August 15, 2002, p. 1.
3. Pritchett, Price, *Carpe Mañana*, Dallas, Pritchett Rummler-Brache, 2000, p. 37.
4. Gibbs, Joe, *Racing to Win*, Sisters, OR, Multnomah Publishers, 2002, with Ken Abraham.
5. Olsen, Milton, *Lessons from Geese*, Lessons from Geese was transcribed from a speech given by Angeles Arrien at the 1991 Organizational Development Network and based on the work of Milton Olsen.

Chapter 40

1. Margaret L. Baptiste, "Exploring Success Through Endurance," *Retirement Life*, April 2002, p. 8.
2. Robinson, Matthew, "President Calvin Coolidge," *Investors Business Daily*, Feb. 13, 1998, p. A1.
3. Carville, John, and Begala, Paul, *Buck Up . . . And Come Back When You Foul Up*, New York, Simon & Schuster, 2001, p. 20.
4. Carville, p. 21.
5. Carville, p. 21.

Chapter 41

1. www.chiefexecutive.net.
2. "Oh, He's Just One of the Help," *South Florida Sun-Sentinel*, June 17, 2002, p. 3.

Chapter 42

1. Speech by Secretary of Education William J. Bennett, The American Sportscasters Dinner, Dec. 3, 1987. See also Bennett, William J., "In Defense of Sports," *Commentary*, Vol. 61, Num. 2, Feb. 1976, p. 32.
2. Bell, Maya, "Chess Kings," *South Florida Sun-Sentinel*, May 28, 2002, p. 1-D.
3. McGrath, Jim, *Heartbeat: George Bush in His Own Words*, New York, Scribner, 2001, p. 264.

4. Harari, Oren, "Lessons from Colin Powell on How to Be a Successful Leader," *Bottom Line Personal*, August 15, 2002, p. 1.

Chapter 43

1. *Entertainment Tonight*, June 7, 2002.
2. Rader, Dotson, "Even the Bad Times Make You Better," *Parade Magazine*, July 28, 2002, p. 6.
3. Schudel, Matt, "Krall Looks for the Story in Music," *South Florida Sun-Sentinel*, May 17, 2002, p. 34.
4. Stolz, Paul, *Adversity Quotient: Turning Obstacles into Opportunites*, New York, Harper Business, 2000, p. 12.

Chapter 45

1. *Pittsburgh Post-Gazette*, September 30, 1999, p. D-4.
2. www.quoteworld.org
3. McGrath, Jim, *Heartbeat: George Bush in His Own Words*, New York, Scribner, 2001, p. 31.

Index

Charles Patrick Garcia— As Speaker

Charles Patrick Garcia is the Chairman and CEO of Sterling Financial Group of Companies. Sterling was named in *Inc* Magazine's Top 500 annual survey (October 2002) as the number eight fastest growing privately-held company in the United States. The company was also named by *Hispanic Business* magazine as the number one fastest growing Hispanic company in the United States and recognized for two years in a row by the University of Florida as the fastest growing privately held company in Florida (2000 and 2001).

Garcia has been labeled a "Jack of All Trades" for his achievements across a range of fields. He is a highly decorated military officer, attorney, community leader, philanthropist, and policy maker. Recently, he has devoted a great deal of time to the important issue of education at both local and national levels. He was appointed by President George W. Bush to the Commission on Educational Excellence for Hispanic Americans, charged with developing a blueprint to close the educational gap for Hispanic children. He is also serving a four-year term as the only Hispanic on Florida's State Board of Education, a new state body responsible for all K-16 education in the state.

He has extensive media experience, having served as Telemundo's military analyst and commentator during the war on Iraq. After the 9/11 attacks, Garcia spoke about creative solutions to the threat of biological weapons on CNN/Crossfire, Fox News, Telemundo, Univision, and other programs.

Garcia frequently speaks in public at keynote, commencement, workshops and other occasions. Garcia uses his own experience as an entrepreneur—who started Sterling Financial with three people in a former broom closet—to motivate others to focus on achievement and success. Garcia's trademark is to touch each person with an inspiring message while providing them with concrete tools they can use everyday.

In his presentations, Garcia offers action steps to help people change their lives or even the direction of their company. Whether it's parents raising children, to high school and college students contemplating their future, to employees considering a career change, people will receive a "Message from Garcia" that inspires them to create an action plan that can change their lives.

For more information visit the *www.successcompass.com* website at *<http://www.successcompass.com>* or call 866-532-3138.